100 Pasta favourites

THE AUSTRALIAN Women's Weekly

contents

Pasta has become such a staple part of our diets now, it is hard to imagine when 'a bowl of pasta' was exotic and very foreign! Here are some of the best ways to serve pasta – not just boiled, but baked in the oven for a delicious lasagne or creamy cannelloni. For that real Italian flavour, stock up with some sun-dried tomatoes, dried porcini mushrooms and grow your own basil on the windowsill to add at the last minute.

Pamela Clark

Food Director

all about pasta

Pasta means paste in Italian, and that's basically all it is: a mixture of coarsely ground durum wheat flour (semolina) and water worked into a dough that's extruded into a variety of shapes and used either fresh or dried. Macaroni and spaghetti are probably the most well known, but there are literally hundreds of different shapes and, to make identification even more difficult, some pasta shapes are known by different names depending on the whim of either the manufacturer or particular region. All pasta shapes are either short or long, and solid or hollow. However, after these two particular classifications, the distinctions seem to get more arbitrary, or even blurred and contradictory.

One rule of thumb in matching pasta shapes and sauces is that the longer and skinnier the pasta, the thinner and wetter the sauce (oil, cream or tomato). The sauce should cling to a pasta that is wound on the tines of a fork. Short, hollow pastas are better with chunky meat or vegetable sauces that get 'trapped' in the cavities, while the delicate, more porous pastas are best served with light, brothy or creamy sauces.

Here is a list of the pasta types we are most familiar with, but it is by no means exhaustive, nor does it mean that these are the only ones you can use to make the recipes in this book – experiment with different shapes until you find the one that seems right to you.

1 angel hair (capelli d'angelo) small, circular nests of very fine, delicate pasta.

2 bucatini (tubular spaghetti) long and hollow like a straw, known as perciatelli in Sicily.

3 elbow macaroni (chifferi) short, small, curved, hollow shape.

4 farfalle (bow ties) also known as butterflies; solid and dense with a frilled edge.

5 fettuccine ribbon pasta slightly wider than tagliolini and thinner than tagliatelle.

6 fettuccine, spinach the green component in the classic paglia e fieno, 'straw and hay' pasta.

7 gnocchi dumplings usually made of potato or semolina; can be boiled, baked or fried.

8 linguine known as flat spaghetti or little tongues because of its shape.

9 macaroni generic name for a wide variety of short and thick hollow pasta.

10 orecchiette (little ears) originally a homemade specialty from Puglia, has a soft centre and chewy rim.

11 pappardelle (or lasagnette) long strips of wide, flat pasta, sometimes with a scalloped edge.

12 penne Italian word for pen; short, straight macaroni cut on the diagonal, either smooth or grooved. Ziti are a fat penne and pennoni are a large variation.

13 ravioli, agnolotti small pasta cases enclosing a savoury or sweet filling.

14 rigatoni large, wide chewy macaroni, usually ridged on the surface.

15 risoni the regional name for a rice-shaped pastina (tiny pasta) that is similar to orzo, stelline and fedelini.

16 shells, large (conchiglie grandi), small (conchiglie) named because they look like conch shells; oblong in shape and pinched at the ends. Available in both grooved and smooth varieties and in many sizes.

17 spaghetti the shape that comes to mind when pasta is mentioned; meaning 'little strands' it is originally from Naples. Spaghettini is a thin version and vermicelli thinner still.

18 spirals, large (fusilli), small (fusillini) corkscrew or spiral-shaped short pasta; a longer variation is called fusilli lunghi; rotini are wider, shorter and has a fatter corkscrew.

19 tagliatelle a long ribbon pasta about 8mm in width; sometimes sold in nests resembling egg noodles.

20 tortellini a pasta ripieni (stuffed pasta) similar to ravioli but made in the shape of a ring or small cap.

perfect pasta

No matter how great your sauce or accompaniments might be, if the pasta isn't of good quality or if it hasn't been cooked properly, the finished dish will not be a success.

1 Bring a large saucepan of water to a rolling boil, allowing approximately 3 litres of water and 1 teaspoon of salt for every 250g pasta. Add pasta to pan and allow water to return to the boil.

2 As soon as pasta becomes pliable enough to bend, stir with a pasta fork to separate strands or pieces. Continue stirring occasionally during cooking. For dried pasta, use the manufacturer's recommended cooking time as a guide, but test 1 to 2 minutes short of the suggested time. The degree of tenderness is very much a matter of personal taste, though most pasta lovers prefer theirs 'al dente', slightly firm to the bite.

3 When cooked, drain the pasta into a large colander over the sink, shaking or swirling colander to make sure all water drains away. Divide pasta among bowls or place in a large serving bowl, add sauce and serve immediately.

To reheat pasta, you can use either of these methods.
Method 1 With pasta still in colander, place over a large saucepan; pour boiling water over pasta, allowing water to drain into pan. Separate pasta pieces with a pasta fork, then lift from colander to drain.
Method 2 After initially draining pasta, allow to cool in a colander until you can handle it. Using your hands, work 2 tablespoons of olive oil through the slightly cooled pasta. Later, when required, reheat pasta by plunging it from the colander into a large saucepan of boiling water, then draining it immediately in the same colander.

A well-stocked pantry and refrigerator enable you to prepare a meal in minutes. You'll always be able to whip up easy pasta dishes in a hurry if you keep ingredients such as these on hand in the fridge or cupboard.

dried pasta of various shapes
    and sizes
vacuum-packed packets of fresh
    lasagne sheets, ravioli, gnocchi, etc.
extra-virgin, virgin and light olive oil
red wine, white wine and
    balsamic vinegars
parmesan, mozzarella and
    pecorino cheeses
bacon, prosciutto and pancetta
eggs
capers, caperberries
black and green olives
anchovies
fresh lemons
sun-dried and semi-dried tomatoes
canned sardines, canned tuna,
    canned salmon
canned tomatoes, tomato puree,
    tomato paste
good-quality bottled tomato pasta
    sauce (sugo)
canned or bottled artichoke hearts
pine nuts, almonds
fresh herbs such as oregano, basil,
    coriander, thyme, etc.
garlic, chillies and onions
fresh salad leaves

angel hair

Also known as capelli d'angelo, angel hair is sold as small, circular nests of very fine, delicate pasta strands; its cooking time is minimal because of its extremely thin nature.

spicy rocket pasta

2 tablespoons olive oil
1 teaspoon dried chilli flakes
2 cloves garlic, crushed
½ teaspoon cracked black pepper
¼ cup (60ml) lemon juice
375g angel hair pasta
80g rocket leaves
2 medium tomatoes (300g), seeded,
   chopped coarsely
⅔ cup firmly packed fresh basil leaves

1 Heat oil in large frying pan; cook chilli and garlic, stirring, until fragrant. Add pepper and juice; stir until hot.
2 Meanwhile, cook pasta in large saucepan of boiling water until tender; drain.
3 Combine chilli mixture and pasta in large bowl with rocket, tomato and basil.

preparation time 10 minutes
cooking time 10 minutes **serves** 4
nutritional count per serving 10.4g total fat
(1.5g saturated fat); 1756kJ (420 cal); 66.4g carbohydrate;
12.1g protein; 4.8g fibre

angel hair pasta with smoked salmon & asparagus

375g angel hair pasta
¼ cup (60ml) olive oil
250g asparagus, trimmed, chopped coarsely
150g smoked salmon, sliced thinly
2 tablespoons rinsed, drained baby capers
⅓ cup finely chopped fresh chives
75g baby rocket leaves
1 lemon, cut into wedges

1 Cook pasta in large saucepan of boiling water until tender; drain. Return pasta to pan.
2 Meanwhile, heat oil in small frying pan; cook asparagus, stirring, until tender.
3 Add asparagus, salmon, capers, chives and rocket to pasta; toss to combine. Serve pasta with lemon wedges.

preparation time 8 minutes
cooking time 5 minutes **serves** 4
nutritional count per serving 16.6g total fat (2.5g saturated fat); 2128kJ (509 cal); 66g carbohydrate; 20.9g protein; 4.7g fibre

hot & sour prawn pasta

1kg cooked medium king prawns
250g angel hair pasta
1 lime
1 lemon
1 medium red capsicum (200g),
    sliced thinly
1 medium yellow capsicum (200g),
    sliced thinly
1 medium red onion (170g), sliced thinly
¼ cup (60ml) olive oil
¼ cup (60ml) rice vinegar
1 tablespoon sambal oelek
1 tablespoon fish sauce
2 tablespoons grated palm sugar
1 cup firmly packed fresh coriander leaves

1 Shell and devein prawns, leaving tails intact.
2 Cook pasta in large saucepan of boiling water
until tender; drain.
3 Meanwhile, halve lime and lemon lengthways; thinly
slice 1 unpeeled half of each, place in large bowl.
Squeeze juice from remaining halves into bowl; add
prawns, pasta and remaining ingredients, toss gently
to combine. Cover; refrigerate 1 hour before serving.

preparation time 30 minutes (plus refrigeration time)
cooking time 5 minutes **serves** 4
nutritional count per serving 15.4g total fat
(2.2g saturated fat); 2159kJ (516 cal); 56g carbohydrate;
35.6g protein; 4.6g fibre

prawn pad thai

600g uncooked medium king prawns
1cm piece fresh ginger (5g), grated
2 cloves garlic, crushed
1 fresh small red thai chilli, sliced thinly
1½ tablespoons grated palm sugar
¼ cup (60ml) soy sauce
2 tablespoons sweet chilli sauce
1 tablespoon fish sauce
1½ tablespoons tomato paste
250g angel hair pasta
1 tablespoon sesame oil
6 green onions, sliced thinly
2 cups (160g) bean sprouts
½ cup loosely packed fresh coriander leaves

1 Shell and devein prawns, leaving tails intact. Place prawns in large bowl with ginger, garlic and chilli; toss to combine. Combine sugar, sauces and paste in screw-top jar; shake well.
2 Cook pasta in large saucepan of boiling water until tender; drain.
3 Meanwhile, heat oil in wok; stir-fry prawn mixture, in batches, until prawns just change colour. Return prawns to wok, add sauce mixture; stir-fry 1 minute or until heated through. Remove from heat; add onion, bean sprouts, coriander and pasta, toss gently to combine.

preparation time 15 minutes
cooking time 10 minutes **serves** 4
nutritional count per serving 6.2g total fat
(0.9g saturated fat); 1597kJ (382 cal); 52.6g carbohydrate; 25.8g protein; 4.9g fibre

angel hair seafood laksa

500g uncooked medium king prawns
1 tablespoon laksa paste
2 cups (500ml) vegetable stock
2 cups (500ml) water
400ml coconut cream
300g firm white fish fillets, chopped coarsely
250g angel hair pasta
300g baby buk choy, chopped coarsely
4 green onions, sliced thinly
¼ cup loosely packed coriander leaves

1 Shell and devein prawns, leaving tails intact.
2 Cook paste in heated large saucepan, stirring, until fragrant. Stir in prawns, stock, the water, coconut cream and fish; bring to the boil. Reduce heat; simmer, uncovered, until prawns change colour and fish is just cooked.
3 Meanwhile, cook pasta in large saucepan of boiling water until tender; drain.
4 While pasta is cooking, stir buk choy, onion and coriander into laksa mixture; cook, uncovered, until buk choy is just wilted.
5 Divide pasta among bowls; top with laksa mixture.

preparation time 10 minutes
cooking time 15 minutes **serves** 4
nutritional count per serving 24.2g total fat (19.1g saturated fat); 2433kJ (582 cal); 48.6g carbohydrate; 39.5g protein; 5.1g fibre

Commercial laksa pastes vary dramatically in their heat intensity so try using less of the laksa paste you've purchased until you can determine how hot it makes the final dish.

fettuccine

Fettuccine, a long, flat, ribbon pasta made of egg and flour, is known as 'little ribbons' in Italian. It is similar to tagliatelle.

chicken pizzaiola with fettuccine

⅓ cup (80ml) olive oil

2 cloves garlic, crushed

½ cup (125ml) dry white wine

½ cup (125ml) chicken stock

2 x 400g cans crushed tomatoes

2 tablespoons coarsely chopped fresh oregano

2 tablespoons coarsely chopped fresh flat-leaf parsley

½ cup (75g) pitted kalamata olives

4 chicken thigh fillets (800g)

¼ cup (35g) plain flour

2 eggs

1 tablespoon milk

1 cup (70g) stale breadcrumbs

7 slices prosciutto (110g)

1¾ cups (175g) grated mozzarella cheese

250g fettuccine pasta

1 Preheat oven to 200°C/180°C fan-forced.

2 Heat half the oil in medium frying pan; cook garlic, stirring, over low heat, until fragrant. Add wine and stock; bring to the boil. Reduce heat; simmer, uncovered, 3 minutes. Add undrained tomatoes, oregano and parsley; bring to the boil. Reduce heat; simmer, uncovered, about 10 minutes or until pizzaiola sauce thickens slightly. Stir in olives.

3 Meanwhile, toss chicken in flour; shake away excess. Dip chicken, one at a time, in combined eggs and milk, then breadcrumbs. Heat remaining oil in large frying pan; cook chicken, in batches, until browned lightly.

4 Place chicken, in single layer, in medium shallow baking dish; top with prosciutto, sauce, then the cheese. Bake, uncovered, in oven about 20 minutes or until chicken is cooked through.

5 Meanwhile, cook pasta in large saucepan of boiling water until tender; drain. Serve pasta topped with chicken pizzaiola.

preparation time 20 minutes
cooking time 40 minutes **serves** 4
nutritional count per serving 46.2g total fat (14.2g saturated fat); 4239kJ (1014 cal); 72.5g carbohydrate; 69.4g protein; 6.1g fibre

fettuccine with creamy tomato & sausage sauce

6 thick italian sausages (720g)
2 cloves garlic, crushed
400g can crushed tomatoes
¼ cup (60ml) dry white wine
300ml cream
375g fettuccine pasta
6 green onions, chopped finely
2 tablespoons fresh sage leaves

1 Cook sausages in heated oiled large frying pan until browned all over and cooked through. Remove sausages from pan; chop coarsely. Cover to keep warm. Drain excess oil from pan.
2 Combine garlic, undrained tomatoes, wine and cream in same pan; bring to the boil. Reduce heat; simmer, uncovered, about 10 minutes or until sauce thickens slightly.
3 Meanwhile, cook pasta in large saucepan of boiling water until tender; drain. Divide among serving bowls.
4 Stir sausage, onion and sage into tomato mixture; spoon sauce over pasta.

preparation time 10 minutes
cooking time 30 minutes **serves** 4
nutritional count per serving 74.8g total fat (41.2g saturated fat); 4794kJ (1147 cal); 76.2g carbohydrate; 37.1g protein; 8.2g fibre

fettuccine with rocket pesto & tomato salsa

500g fettuccine pasta
8 cloves garlic, quartered
½ cup coarsely chopped fresh basil
120g rocket leaves, chopped coarsely
⅔ cup (160ml) olive oil
½ cup (40g) finely grated parmesan cheese
3 medium tomatoes (450g), chopped coarsely
2 tablespoons lemon juice
2 fresh small red thai chillies, sliced thinly
⅓ cup (50g) roasted pine nuts

1 Cook pasta in large saucepan of boiling water until tender; drain.
2 Meanwhile, blend or process garlic, basil, rocket and oil until smooth.
3 Combine pasta, rocket pesto, cheese, tomato, juice and chilli in large saucepan; stir, over medium heat, until hot. Add nuts; toss gently to combine.

preparation time 10 minutes
cooking time 15 minutes **serves** 4
nutritional count per serving 50.1g total fat (8g saturated fat); 3779kJ (904 cal); 88.9g carbohydrate; 21.1g protein; 7.3g fibre

You could substitute baby spinach leaves for the rocket to give a milder-flavoured pesto.

fettuccine carbonara

500g fettuccine pasta
6 rindless bacon rashers (390g), sliced thinly
100g button mushrooms, sliced thinly
300ml cream
4 eggs, beaten lightly
1 cup (80g) coarsely grated parmesan cheese

1 Cook pasta in large saucepan of boiling water until tender; drain. Return pasta to pan; cover to keep warm.
2 Meanwhile, cook bacon in large frying pan, stirring, until crisp. Add mushrooms; cook, stirring, until tender. Add cream; stir until heated through.
3 Working quickly, gently combine bacon mixture, hot pasta and combined egg and cheese. Serve topped with fresh oregano leaves, if you like.

preparation time 5 minutes
cooking time 15 minutes **serves** 4
nutritional count per serving 57.6g total fat
(31.9g saturated fat); 3407kJ (815 cal); 33.5g carbohydrate;
40.4g protein; 2.9g fibre

fettuccine alfredo

375g fettuccine pasta
90g butter, chopped coarsely
⅔ cup (160ml) cream
1 cup (80g) finely grated parmesan cheese
2 tablespoons finely chopped fresh flat-leaf parsley

1 Cook pasta in large saucepan of boiling water until tender; drain. Return pasta to pan; cover to keep warm.
2 Meanwhile, stir butter and cream in medium saucepan over low heat until butter melts and combines well with the cream; remove from heat. Add cheese; stir until sauce is blended and smooth.
3 Pour sauce over hot pasta, toss well; sprinkle with parsley to serve.

preparation time 5 minutes
cooking time 15 minutes **serves** 4
nutritional count per serving 43.3g total fat
(27.9g saturated fat); 3056kJ (731 cal); 65.3g carbohydrate;
19.1g protein; 3.2g fibre

pagli e fieno

2 teaspoons olive oil
5 green onions, sliced thinly
2 cloves garlic, crushed
500g button mushrooms, sliced thickly
1 tablespoon dry white wine
1¼ cups (310ml) cream
¼ cup coarsely chopped fresh flat-leaf parsley
150g plain fettuccine pasta
150g spinach-flavoured fettuccine pasta

1 Cook both pastas in large saucepan of boiling water until tender; drain.
2 Meanwhile, heat oil in medium saucepan; cook onion and garlic, stirring, until onion softens. Add mushrooms; cook, stirring, until just browned. Add wine and cream; bring to the boil. Reduce heat; simmer, uncovered, about 5 minutes or until sauce thickens slightly. Stir in parsley.
3 Toss pasta in large bowl with sauce.

preparation time 10 minutes
cooking time 15 minutes **serves** 4
nutritional count per serving 37.1g total fat
(22.6g saturated fat); 2650kJ (634 cal); 56.3g carbohydrate; 15g protein; 6.7g fibre

fettuccine boscaiola

2 teaspoons olive oil
200g button mushrooms, sliced thickly
2 cloves garlic, crushed
200g shaved ham, chopped coarsely
¼ cup (60ml) dry white wine
1¼ cups (310ml) cream
500g fettuccine pasta
2 tablespoons coarsely chopped fresh chives

1 Cook pasta in large saucepan of boiling water until tender; drain.
2 Meanwhile, heat oil in large saucepan; cook mushrooms, garlic and ham, stirring, until ingredients are browned lightly. Add wine; boil, uncovered, until wine reduces by half.
3 Add cream to mushroom mixture; reduce heat. Simmer, uncovered, until sauce thickens slightly.
4 Add chives and pasta to sauce; toss to combine.

preparation time 10 minutes
cooking time 20 minutes **serves** 4
nutritional count per serving 38.1g total fat
(22.7g saturated fat); 3436kJ (822 cal); 87.8g carbohydrate; 26.8g protein; 5.7g fibre

fettuccine alle vongole

2 tablespoons olive oil
3 cloves garlic, crushed
1 fresh long red chilli, chopped finely
1 tablespoon rinsed, drained baby capers
¾ cup (180ml) dry white wine
¾ cup (180ml) fish stock
2 tablespoons lemon juice
1kg clams
375g fettuccine pasta
½ cup coarsely chopped fresh flat-leaf parsley
¼ cup coarsely chopped fresh chives

1 Heat oil in large saucepan; cook garlic and chilli, stirring, 1 minute. Add capers, wine, stock and juice; bring to the boil. Add clams; cook, covered, about 5 minutes or until clams open (discard any that do not).
2 Meanwhile, cook pasta in large saucepan of boiling water until tender; drain.
3 Add pasta and herbs to clam mixture; toss gently to combine.

preparation time 15 minutes
cooking time 15 minutes **serves** 4
nutritional count per serving 10.5g total fat (1.6g saturated fat); 2002kJ (479 cal); 65.9g carbohydrate; 20.2g protein; 4g fibre

A classic Italian pasta, alle vongole (Italian for 'clams') is usually made with tiny baby clams, but you can use any clams you like for this recipe.

fettuccine with meatballs

500g lean beef mince
1 cup (70g) stale breadcrumbs
2 tablespoons finely chopped fresh flat-leaf parsley
2 tablespoons finely chopped fresh chives
1 egg
1 teaspoon worcestershire sauce
2 teaspoons olive oil
500g fettuccine pasta
rosemary paprika sauce
810g canned crushed tomatoes
2 cup (500ml) water
⅓ cup (40ml) dry red wine
2 medium brown onions (300g), chopped finely
1 teaspoon worcestershire sauce
2 teaspoons sweet paprika
6 sprigs fresh rosemary

1 Make rosemary paprika sauce.
2 Combine beef, breadcrumbs, parsley, chives, egg and sauce in large bowl; shape into small meatballs.
3 Heat oil in medium saucepan; cook meatballs, in batches, until browned all over and cooked through. Drain on absorbent paper.
4 Meanwhile, cook pasta in large saucepan of boiling water until tender; drain.
5 Add meatballs to sauce; mix well. Stir until heated through. Serve pasta with meatballs and sauce.
rosemary paprika sauce Combine ingredients in large saucepan; bring to the boil. Reduce heat; simmer, uncovered, about 20 minutes or until thickened slightly.

preparation time 15 minutes
cooking time 45 minutes **serves** 4
nutritional count per serving 34.1g total fat (8.4g saturated fat); 3984kJ (953 cal); 108.8g carbohydrate; 44.2g protein; 8.6g fibre

salmon fettuccine in creamy lime sauce

375g fettuccine pasta
1 tablespoon olive oil
4 x 220g salmon fillets, skinned
1 small brown onion (80g), chopped finely
1 clove garlic, crushed
2 teaspoons finely grated lime rind
1 tablespoon lime juice
¼ cup (60ml) dry white wine
300ml cream
½ teaspoon drained pink peppercorns, crushed
⅓ cup coarsely chopped fresh chives

1 Cook pasta in large saucepan of boiling water until tender; drain.
2 Meanwhile, heat half the oil in large frying pan; cook fish until browned both sides and cooked as desired. Place fish in large bowl; flake into large pieces.
3 Heat remaining oil in same pan; cook onion and garlic, stirring, until onion softens. Add rind, juice and wine; bring to the boil. Boil, stirring, until liquid reduces to about 2 tablespoons. Stir in cream and peppercorns; return to the boil. Remove from heat.
4 Combine pasta and chives in large bowl with fish, drizzle with sauce; toss gently.

preparation time 20 minutes
cooking time 25 minutes **serves** 4
nutritional count per serving 53.7g total fat (25.8g saturated fat); 4138kJ (990 cal); 67.5g carbohydrate; 55.3g protein; 3.7g fibre

veal escalopes with rocket & pistachio pesto

600g piece veal rump, sliced thinly
1 tablespoon olive oil
¼ cup (60ml) dry white wine
2 teaspoons finely grated lemon rind
1 clove garlic, crushed
375g fettuccine pasta
rocket & pistachio pesto
50g baby rocket leaves, trimmed
½ cup (70g) pistachios, roasted
⅓ cup (25g) coarsely grated parmesan cheese
1 clove garlic, quartered
1 tablespoon lemon juice
¾ cup (180ml) olive oil

1 Combine veal, oil, wine, rind and garlic in medium bowl. Cover; refrigerate 2 hours.
2 Make rocket & pistachio pesto.
3 Cook pasta in large saucepan of boiling water until tender; drain.
4 Meanwhile, cook veal, in batches, under preheated grill until browned all over and cooked as desired.
5 Combine pasta in large bowl with half the pesto; toss gently. Serve veal on pasta topped with remaining pesto.
rocket & pistachio pesto Blend or process rocket, nuts, cheese and garlic until well combined. With motor operating, gradually add combined juice and oil in a thin steady stream; blend until pesto thickens slightly.

preparation time 10 minutes (plus refrigeration time)
cooking time 15 minutes **serves** 4
nutritional count per serving 58.9g total fat (9.4g saturated fat); 4239kJ (1014 cal); 67g carbohydrate; 49.9g protein; 5g fibre

fettuccine veal goulash

400g veal fillet
2 teaspoons olive oil
1 medium brown onion (150g), sliced finely
2 cloves garlic, crushed
1 teaspoon sweet paprika
1½ cups (375ml) beef stock
2 tablespoons sour cream
1 tablespoon lemon juice
1 tablespoon wholegrain mustard
375g fettuccine pasta
250g spinach, trimmed, shredded coarsely
1 tablespoon fresh dill

1 Cook veal in heated heated oiled large frying pan until browned and cooked as desired. Stand 5 minutes before cutting into thin slices; cover to keep warm.
2 Heat oil in same pan; cook onion, garlic and paprika, stirring, until onion softens. Add stock; bring to the boil. Reduce heat; simmer, uncovered, 5 minutes. Add sour cream, juice and mustard; cook, stirring, 1 minute.
3 Meanwhile, cook pasta in large saucepan of boiling water until tender; drain. Place pasta, spinach and dill in large bowl with veal goulash; toss gently.

preparation time 15 minutes
cooking time 15 minutes **serves** 4
nutritional count per serving 9.3g total fat
(3.7g saturated fat); 2136kJ (511 cal); 67.5g carbohydrate; 35.8g protein; 4.9g fibre

beef & red wine casserole

2 cups (500ml) water
1kg skirt steak, trimmed, cut into 3cm cubes
2 medium brown onions (300g), sliced thickly
2 tablespoons olive oil
6 cloves garlic, crushed
2 cups (500ml) beef stock
2 cups (500ml) dry red wine
½ cup (140g) tomato paste
1 tablespoon finely chopped fresh rosemary
1 tablespoon finely chopped fresh flat-leaf parsley
500g fresh fettuccine pasta

1 Combine the water, steak, onion, oil, garlic, stock, wine and paste in deep 3-litre (12-cup) microwave-safe dish; cook, covered, on HIGH (100%) for 50 minutes, stirring every 15 minutes to ensure steak remains covered in liquid. Uncover; cook on HIGH (100%) about 10 minutes or until steak is tender. Stir in herbs.
2 During final 10 minutes of casserole cooking time, cook pasta in large saucepan of boiling water until tender; drain.
3 Divide pasta among serving dishes; top with beef and sauce.

preparation time 20 minutes
cooking time 1 hour **serves** 4
nutritional count per serving 16.3g total fat (4.1g saturated fat); 3010kJ (720 cal); 51.5g carbohydrate; 67.5g protein; 5.3g fibre

gnocchi

From the Italian word for dumplings, gnocchi are little balls of dough – great for soaking up delicious pasta sauces.

gnocchi with tomato & basil sauce

1 litre (4 cups) milk
1 cup (160g) semolina
4 egg yolks
⅔ cup (50g) finely grated parmesan cheese
2 tablespoons semolina, extra
2 tablespoons olive oil
4 cloves garlic, crushed
½ cup coarsely chopped fresh basil
2 cups (520g) bottled tomato pasta sauce
40g butter, melted
½ cup (40g) finely grated parmesan cheese, extra

1 Bring milk to the boil in medium saucepan. Gradually add semolina, stirring constantly. Reduce heat; simmer, stirring, about 5 minutes or until mixture thickens. Remove from heat; stir in egg yolks and cheese. Stand 5 minutes.
2 Sprinkle extra semolina on flat surface; roll mixture into two 5cm-thick sausage shapes. Wrap in plastic; refrigerate 1 hour or until firm.
3 Meanwhile, heat oil in small saucepan; cook garlic and basil, stirring, until fragrant. Add pasta sauce; bring to the boil. Reduce heat; simmer, covered, 2 minutes.
4 Preheat grill. Cut semolina into 2cm gnocchi pieces. Place gnocchi, in single layer, on oiled oven trays. Brush gnocchi with melted butter; sprinkle with extra cheese. Grill about 3 minutes or until cheese browns lightly.
5 Serve gnocchi topped with tomato sauce; sprinkle with fresh basil leaves, if desired.

preparation time 15 minutes (plus refrigeration time)
cooking time 15 minutes **serves** 6
nutritional count per serving 27.9g total fat (13.2g saturated fat); 2069kJ (495 cal); 40.9g carbohydrate; 18.8g protein; 3.3g fibre

gnocchi with caramelised pumpkin & sage sauce

500g butternut pumpkin, cut into 1cm cubes
¼ cup (60ml) chicken stock (*see note, below*)
1 large leek (500g), sliced thinly
1 tablespoon brown sugar
1½ cups (375ml) water
2 teaspoons finely chopped fresh sage
½ cup (125ml) low-fat evaporated milk
1kg fresh potato gnocchi

1 Preheat oven to 220°C/200°C fan-forced.
2 Place pumpkin in oiled baking dish; bake, uncovered, about 30 minutes or until pumpkin is tender.
3 Bring stock to the boil in large saucepan, add leek; cook, stirring, until leek softens. Add pumpkin and sugar; cook, stirring, about 10 minutes or until pumpkin caramelises. Stir in the water, sage and milk; blend or process pumpkin mixture, in batches, until smooth. Return pumpkin sauce to same pan; stir over heat until hot.
4 Meanwhile, cook gnocchi in large saucepan of boiling water until they float to the surface and are just tender; drain. Toss hot gnocchi through hot pumpkin sauce.

preparation time 15 minutes
cooking time 40 minutes **serves** 4
nutritional count per serving 1.7g total fat (0.5g saturated fat); 1760kJ (421 cal); 79.3g carbohydrate; 16.9g protein; 8.2g fibre

To make this a meal suitable for vegetarians, substitute vegetable stock for the chicken stock. Fresh potato gnocchi is available from the refrigerated section of most supermarkets.

crumbed veal cutlets with gnocchi in mushroom sauce

2 eggs, beaten lightly
2 tablespoons milk
¼ cup (35g) plain flour
¾ cup (75g) packaged breadcrumbs
¾ cup (50g) stale breadcrumbs
¾ cup (75g) pizza cheese
½ cup coarsely chopped fresh flat-leaf parsley
8 veal cutlets (1kg)
¼ cup (60ml) olive oil
2 cloves garlic, sliced thinly
250g button mushrooms, sliced thinly
¾ cup (180ml) cream
½ cup (125ml) beef stock
625g fresh potato gnocchi

1 Whisk egg, milk and flour in medium bowl. Combine crumbs, cheese and ⅓ cup of the parsley in another bowl. Coat cutlets in egg mixture then cheese mixture. Place cutlets, in single layer, on tray; refrigerate 10 minutes.
2 Heat half the oil in large frying pan; cook cutlets until browned both sides and cooked as desired. Cover.
3 Heat remaining oil in same pan; cook garlic and mushrooms, stirring, until just tender. Add cream and stock; bring to the boil. Reduce heat; simmer, stirring, until sauce thickens slightly.
4 Meanwhile, cook gnocchi in large saucepan of boiling water until they float to the surface and are just tender; drain, place in large bowl. Stir remaining parsley into sauce and pour over gnocchi; toss to combine. Serve gnocchi with cutlets.

preparation time 15 minutes
cooking time 35 minutes **serves** 4
nutritional count per serving 47.1g total fat (20.6g saturated fat); 3992kJ (955 cal); 62.4g carbohydrate; 67g protein; 6.6g fibre

gnocchi al quattro formaggi

¼ cup (60ml) dry white wine
1 cup (250g) mascarpone cheese
1 cup (100g) coarsely grated mozzarella cheese
½ cup (40g) coarsely grated parmesan cheese
¼ cup (60ml) milk
625g fresh potato gnocchi
75g gorgonzola cheese, crumbled

1 Add wine to large saucepan; bring to the boil. Boil, uncovered, until wine reduces by half. Reduce heat, add mascarpone; stir until mixture is smooth. Add mozzarella, parmesan and milk; cook, stirring, until cheeses melt and sauce is smooth.
2 Meanwhile, cook gnocchi in large saucepan of boiling water until they float to the surface and are tender; drain.
3 Add gnocchi and gorgonzola to sauce; toss gently.

preparation time 10 minutes
cooking time 10 minutes **serves** 4
nutritional count per serving 59.5g total fat (39.1g saturated fat); 3285kJ (786 cal); 28.8g carbohydrate; 32g protein; 2.2g fibre

Serve this pasta dish with grilled chops or poached fish fillets for a delicious main meal.

gnocchi with roasted pumpkin & burnt butter sauce

500g trimmed pumpkin, cut into 1cm cubes
1kg fresh potato gnocchi
100g butter
1 tablespoon olive oil
1 clove garlic, crushed
1 tablespoon finely shredded fresh sage

1 Preheat oven to 180°C/160°C fan-forced.
2 Place pumpkin on oiled oven tray; roast about 15 minutes or until just tender.
3 Cook gnocchi in large saucepan of boiling water until they float to the surface and are just tender; drain.
4 Meanwhile, melt butter with oil in medium frying pan; cook garlic, stirring, 2 minutes. Add sage; cook, stirring, until butter foams.
5 Combine pumpkin, gnocchi and butter mixture in large bowl; stir gently.

preparation time 5 minutes
cooking time 15 minutes **serves** 4
nutritional count per serving 27.8g total fat (15.5g saturated fat); 2692kJ (644 cal); 81g carbohydrate; 13.3g protein; 7.4g fibre

You will need to buy a piece of unpeeled pumpkin weighing about 650g for this recipe.

lasagne & cannelloni

This classic Italian dish of layers of pasta, meat and cheese sauce is the ideal recipe to make when you're entertaining as most of the work can be done well in advance.

four cheese lasagne

2 teaspoons olive oil
1 medium brown onion (150g), chopped finely
2 cloves garlic, crushed
500g lean beef mince
2 x 425g cans crushed tomatoes
½ cup (140g) tomato paste
½ teaspoon white sugar
½ cup finely chopped fresh basil
¼ cup finely chopped fresh oregano
500g ricotta cheese
1 cup (80g) finely grated parmesan cheese
1 cup (100g) coarsely grated mozzarella cheese
¼ teaspoon ground nutmeg
4 eggs
200g large instant lasagne sheets
1 cup (100g) pizza cheese

1 Heat oil in large saucepan; cook onion and garlic, stirring, until onion softens. Add mince; cook, stirring, until mince changes colour. Add undrained tomatoes, paste and sugar; cook, stirring, until sauce thickens. Remove from heat; stir in basil and oregano.
2 Preheat oven to 180°C/160°C fan-forced.
3 Beat ricotta, parmesan, mozzarella and nutmeg in medium bowl with electric mixer until well combined. Add eggs, one at a time, beating until just combined between additions.
4 Place a third of the lasagne sheets in shallow 2.5-litre (10-cup) baking dish; top with half the meat sauce and half the cheese mixture. Top with another third of the lasagne sheets, remaining meat sauce, remaining lasagne sheets then remaining cheese mixture. Top with pizza cheese.
5 Bake, uncovered, about 45 minutes or until cheese browns lightly. Stand lasagne 5 minutes before serving.

preparation time 25 minutes
cooking time 55 minutes **serves** 6
nutritional count per serving 32.7g total fat
(17.2g saturated fat); 2671kJ (639 cal); 33.2g carbohydrate; 50.9g protein; 4.1g fibre

chicken & leek lasagne

60g butter
1 large leek (500g), sliced thinly
¼ cup (35g) plain flour
2 teaspoons dijon mustard
2 cups (500ml) chicken stock, warmed
3 cups (480g) shredded barbecued chicken
4 fresh lasagne sheets (200g), trimmed to
    fit baking dish
⅔ cup (80g) coarsely grated cheddar cheese

1 Preheat oven to 180°C/160°C fan-forced.
2 Melt butter in medium saucepan; cook leek, stirring,
until soft. Add flour; cook, stirring, until mixture thickens
and bubbles. Gradually stir in mustard and stock; stir
over medium heat until mixture boils and thickens.
Reserve ⅔ cup of the sauce, then stir chicken into
remaining sauce.
3 Oil shallow 2-litre (8-cup) baking dish. Cover base
with one lasagne sheet; top with about a quarter of the
warm chicken mixture. Repeat layering with remaining
lasagne and chicken mixture, finishing with chicken
mixture; top with reserved sauce and the cheese.
4 Bake, covered, in oven, 30 minutes; uncover, bake
about 20 minutes or until browned lightly. Stand
5 minutes before serving.

preparation time 25 minutes
cooking time 1 hour 10 minutes **serves** 4
nutritional count per serving 24.8g total fat
(8.5g saturated fat); 1685kJ (403 cal);
15.5g carbohydrate; 28.8g protein; 2.4g fibre

**You need to buy a large barbecued chicken
weighing approximately 900g for this recipe.**

tuna spinach lasagne

20g butter
2 tablespoons plain flour
1 cup milk
¾ cup (90g) coarsely grated cheddar cheese
4 fresh lasagne sheets (200g), trimmed to
    fit baking dish
1 cup (70g) stale breadcrumbs
tuna spinach mornay
50g butter
1 medium brown onion (150g), sliced thinly
¼ cup (35g) plain flour
2 cups (500ml) milk, warmed
150g baby spinach leaves
425g can tuna in springwater, drained
2 tablespoons lemon juice

1 Preheat oven to 180°C/160°C fan-forced. Oil shallow
2-litre (8-cup) baking dish. Make tuna spinach mornay.
2 Melt butter in small saucepan. Add flour; cook, stirring,
until mixture thickens. Gradually stir in milk over medium
heat until mixture boils. Stir in a quarter of the cheese.
3 Line dish with one lasagne sheet; top with a third of
the mornay. Repeat layering with lasagne and mornay,
finishing with lasagne. Spread cheese sauce over top;
sprinkle with breadcrumbs and remaining cheese.
4 Bake, covered, 30 minutes; uncover, bake about
20 minutes or until browned lightly. Stand 5 minutes.
tuna spinach mornay Melt butter in pan; cook onion
until soft. Add flour; cook, stirring, until mixture thickens.
Gradually add milk; stir until mixture boils and thickens.
Remove from heat; stir in spinach, tuna and juice.

preparation time 25 minutes
cooking time 1 hour 10 minutes **serves** 4
nutritional count per serving 21.7g total fat
(13.4g saturated fat); 1789kJ (428 cal);
30.9g carbohydrate; 26.2g protein; 2.5g fibre

lasagne with pesto

15g butter
¼ cup (40g) pine nuts
1 cup firmly packed fresh basil leaves
1 clove garlic, crushed
2 tablespoons grated parmesan cheese
1 teaspoon white sugar
½ cup (125ml) olive oil
375g fresh lasagne sheets, sliced thickly

1 Melt butter in small saucepan. Cook nuts, stirring over medium heat, until browned lightly; cool.
2 Process basil, nuts, garlic, cheese and sugar until smooth. While motor is operating, gradually add oil in a thin stream; process until combined.
3 Cook pasta in large saucepan of boiling water until tender; drain.
4 Stir pesto through pasta to serve.

preparation time 10 minutes
cooking time 15 minutes **serves** 4
nutritional count per serving 39.6g total fat (6.6g saturated fat); 2846kJ (681 cal); 67.6g carbohydrate; 12g protein; 4g fibre

Pesto can be made a week ahead; refrigerate, covered, or freeze for up to three months.

wonton lasagne stacks

600g beef mince
2 tablespoons tomato paste
2 green onions, chopped finely
2 eggs
250g ricotta cheese
2 tablespoons finely shredded fresh basil
12 wonton wrappers
½ cup (50g) pizza cheese
700g bottled tomato pasta sauce

1 Preheat oven to 180°C/160°C fan-forced.
2 Combine mince, paste, onion and one egg in medium bowl; shape mixture into eight patties.
3 Combine ricotta, basil and remaining egg in another medium bowl.
4 Place four wrappers, in single layer, in shallow baking dish; top each with a pattie. Divide half the ricotta mixture among patties; sprinkle with half the pizza cheese, top with a wrapper; repeat layering ending with a wrapper.
5 Pour sauce over stacks; cook about 50 minutes or until stacks are cooked through and set. Serve with crusty Italian bread and a green salad, if desired.

preparation time 20 minutes
cooking time 1 hour **serves** 4
nutritional count per serving 27.8g total fat (13.3g saturated fat); 2178kJ (521 cal); 19.3g carbohydrate; 46.8g protein; 3.8g fibre

lasagne with tomato sauce

375g fresh lasagne sheets, sliced thickly
2 tablespoons extra virgin olive oil
6 medium tomatoes (900g), peeled, seeded,
    chopped coarsely
¼ cup coarsely chopped fresh basil
2 cloves garlic, crushed
2 teaspoons red wine vinegar
1 fresh small red thai chilli, chopped finely
80g low-fat fetta cheese, crumbled

1 Cook pasta in large saucepan of boiling water until tender; drain. Sprinkle half the oil over pasta; toss gently.
2 Combine tomato, basil, garlic, remaining oil, vinegar and chilli in medium bowl.
3 Divide pasta among serving plates. Spoon tomato mixture over pasta; sprinkle with cheese.

preparation time 15 minutes
cooking time 5 minutes **serves** 8
nutritional count per serving 6.7g total fat
(1.7g saturated fat); 1003kJ (240 cal); 34.2g carbohydrate;
9g protein; 3.1g fibre

To peel tomatoes, slice a cross in the bottom of each tomato, then place in a large bowl of boiling water for 1 minute; drain. Rinse under cold water; peel.

smoked salmon lasagne

8 sheets curly lasagne
400g thinly sliced smoked salmon
1 medium avocado (250g), sliced thinly
⅓ cup (80ml) lime juice
½ cup (125ml) peanut oil
1 tablespoon finely chopped fresh dill
2 teaspoons wholegrain mustard
100g baby spinach leaves

1 Cook pasta in large saucepan of boiling water until tender; drain. Rinse under cold water; drain, then pat dry with absorbent paper.
2 Place two pasta sheets on board; layer half the salmon evenly over sheets. Top salmon with pasta sheets then avocado, pasta sheets, remaining salmon and remaining pasta sheets. Cut stacks in half, then cut in half diagonally. Place two pieces on each serving plate.
3 Place juice, oil, dill and mustard in screw-top jar; shake well. Pour half the dressing over spinach in medium bowl; toss gently. Drizzle stacks with remaining dressing; serve with spinach.

preparation time 15 minutes
cooking time 10 minutes **serves** 4
nutritional count per serving 43.5g total fat
(8.3g saturated fat); 2583kJ (618 cal); 27.4g carbohydrate;
28.9g protein; 2.7g fibre

classic lasagne

1 tablespoon olive oil
1 medium brown onion (150g), chopped finely
1 medium carrot (120g), chopped finely
1 stalk celery (150g), trimmed, chopped finely
2 cloves garlic, crushed
500g beef mince
⅓ cup (80ml) dry red wine
850g can crushed tomatoes
2 tablespoons tomato paste
½ cup (125ml) water
4 slices prosciutto (60g), chopped finely
1 tablespoon coarsely chopped fresh oregano
2 tablespoons coarsely chopped fresh flat-leaf parsley
18 instant lasagne sheets
½ cup (40g) grated parmesan cheese
cheese sauce
60g butter
⅓ cup (50g) plain flour
1 litre (4 cups) milk
¾ cup (60g) grated parmesan cheese
pinch ground nutmeg

1 Heat oil in large frying pan; cook onion, carrot, celery and garlic, stirring, until onion is soft. Add beef; cook, stirring, until browned. Add wine; bring to the boil. Stir in undrained tomatoes, paste and the water; reduce heat. Simmer, uncovered, about 1 hour or until mixture is thick. Stir in prosciutto and herbs; cool slightly.
2 Meanwhile, make cheese sauce.
3 Preheat oven to 180°C/160°C fan-forced. Oil shallow 3-litre (12-cup) ovenproof dish.
4 Place six lasagne sheets into prepared dish. Spread with half the meat sauce; drizzle with 1 cup of the cheese sauce. Repeat layering; top with remaining pasta sheets then spread with remaining cheese sauce and sprinkle with cheese.
5 Bake about 45 minutes or until pasta is tender and cheese is browned lightly.
cheese sauce Melt butter in heated large saucepan, add flour; cook, stirring, until mixture bubbles and thickens. Remove from heat; gradually stir in milk. Cook, stirring, until mixture boils and thickens. Remove from heat; stir in cheese and nutmeg. Cool 10 minutes.

preparation time 40 minutes
cooking time 2 hours 10 minutes **serves** 6
nutritional count per serving 32.5g total fat
(17.2g saturated fat); 2993kJ (716 cal); 62g carbohydrate; 38.7g protein; 5.6g fibre

Recipe can be made up to three days ahead; store, covered, in the refrigerator. Recipe can also be frozen for up to three months.

eggplant, tomato & leek lasagne

3 medium eggplants (900g)
coarse cooking salt
1 large brown onion (200g), chopped finely
4 cloves garlic, crushed
3 large tomatoes (660g), chopped coarsely
2 tablespoons tomato paste
¼ cup finely shredded fresh basil leaves
1 tablespoon butter
2 medium leeks (700g), chopped finely
2 tablespoons white sugar
4 fresh lasagne sheets (200g), trimmed to
    fit 19cm-square ovenproof dish
1 cup (120g) grated cheddar cheese

1 Cut eggplants lengthways into 1cm slices; place in colander, sprinkle with salt, stand 30 minutes. Rinse; drain, pat dry. Cook in heated oiled large saucepan until browned.
2 Cook onion and half the garlic in same pan, stirring, until onion softens. Stir in tomato, paste and basil; simmer, uncovered, about 20 minutes or until thickened slightly. Blend or process tomato mixture until just combined.
3 Melt butter in same pan, add leek and remaining garlic; cook, stirring, until leek is soft. Add sugar; cook, stirring, about 5 minutes or until leek is browned lightly.
4 Preheat oven to 200°C/180°C fan-forced. Oil deep 19cm-square (10-cup) ovenproof dish.
5 Position one pasta sheet in base of dish; top with a quarter of the eggplant, a quarter of the leek mixture, a quarter of the tomato mixture and a quarter of the cheese. Repeat layers three times, ending with cheese. Bake, uncovered, 50 minutes.

preparation time 40 minutes (plus standing time)
cooking time 1 hour 30 minutes **serves** 6
nutritional count per serving 10.7g total fat (6.1g saturated fat); 1392kJ (333 cal); 40.6g carbohydrate; 13.8g protein; 9.1g fibre

ricotta & silver beet lasagne

1kg silver beet, trimmed
3 eggs, beaten lightly
2 cups (480g) ricotta cheese
¼ cup (20g) coarsely grated parmesan cheese
3 green onions, chopped finely
1½ cups (390ml) bottled tomato pasta sauce
12 sheets instant lasagne
1 cup (120g) coarsely grated cheddar cheese

1 Preheat oven to 180°C/160°C fan-forced. Oil shallow 3-litre (12-cup) ovenproof dish.
2 Boil, steam or microwave silver beet until just wilted; drain. Squeeze as much liquid as possible from silver beet; chop coarsely. Combine egg, ricotta, parmesan and onion in large bowl; stir in silver beet.
3 Spread half the pasta sauce over base of ovenproof dish. Cover with three lasagne sheets; top with a third of the silver beet mixture. Cover silver beet layer with three lasagne sheets; repeat layering with remaining silver beet mixture and remaining lasagne sheets. Top lasagne with remaining sauce; sprinkle with cheddar.
4 Cover lasagne with foil; bake 40 minutes. Remove foil; bake a further 20 minutes or until top is browned.

preparation time 40 minutes
cooking time 1 hour 5 minutes **serves** 4
nutritional count per serving 30.9g total fat
(17.6g saturated fat); 2742kJ (656 cal); 53.6g carbohydrate;
37.1g protein; 7.6g fibre

chicken & prosciutto cannelloni

50g butter
¼ cup (35g) plain flour
⅔ cup (160ml) milk
1½ cups (375ml) chicken stock
½ cup (40g) grated parmesan cheese
400g grated mozzarella cheese
1 tablespoon olive oil
2 medium brown onions (300g), chopped finely
3 cloves garlic, crushed
1kg chicken mince
2 tablespoons finely chopped fresh sage
850g can crushed tomatoes
½ cup (125ml) dry white wine
¼ cup (70g) tomato paste
3 teaspoons white sugar
12 fresh lasagne sheets
24 slices prosciutto (360g), cut in half crossways

Pancetta or double-smoked ham can be substituted for the prosciutto.

1 Melt butter in medium saucepan, add flour; cook, stirring, until mixture thickens and bubbles. Gradually stir in milk and stock; cook, stirring, until sauce boils and thickens. Remove from heat; stir in parmesan and a quarter of the mozzarella.

2 Heat oil in large saucepan; cook onion and garlic, stirring, until onion is soft. Add chicken; cook, stirring, until browned. Stir in sage. Combine chicken and cheese sauce in large bowl; cool.

3 Combine undrained crushed tomatoes, wine, paste and sugar in same large pan; cook, stirring, 10 minutes. Cool 10 minutes; blend or process, in batches, until smooth.

4 Preheat oven to 180°C/160°C fan-forced.

5 Cut pasta sheets in half crossways. Place two pieces of prosciutto on each piece of pasta. Top each with ¼ cup chicken mixture; roll to enclose filling. Repeat with remaining pasta, prosciutto and chicken mixture.

6 Oil two 3-litre (12-cup) ovenproof dishes. Pour a quarter of the tomato sauce into base of each dish; place half the pasta rolls, seam-side down, in each dish. Pour remaining tomato sauce over rolls; sprinkle with remaining mozzarella.

7 Bake cannelloni, covered, 30 minutes. Uncover, bake a further 15 minutes or until cheese melts and browns. Serve with a green salad, if you like.

preparation time 30 minutes
cooking time 1 hour 10 minutes **serves** 8
nutritional count per serving 36g total fat (18.5g saturated fat); 2746kJ (657 cal); 25.3g carbohydrate; 54.1g protein; 3.2g fibre

linguine

Linguine ('little tongues') are flat strands of pasta related to fettuccine, but thinner and narrower. Spaghetti, bucatini or fettuccine can be used in place of the linguine.

linguine & chorizo in creamy mushroom sauce

300g swiss brown mushrooms, halved
2 tablespoons olive oil
2 cloves garlic, crushed
2 chorizo sausages (340g)
½ cup (125ml) dry white wine
1 cup (250ml) chicken stock
300g sour cream
4 green onions, chopped finely
375g linguine pasta
2 tablespoons finely shredded fresh basil

1 Preheat oven to 240°C/220°C fan-forced.
2 Place mushrooms in large shallow baking dish, drizzle with combined oil and garlic; roast, uncovered, about 15 minutes or until mushrooms are browned and tender.
3 Meanwhile, cook chorizo in heated medium frying pan until browned and cooked through; drain on absorbent paper, chop coarsely.
4 Place wine in same cleaned pan; bring to the boil. Reduce heat; simmer, uncovered, 5 minutes. Stir in stock and sour cream; return mixture to the boil. Reduce heat; simmer, uncovered, about 2 minutes or until sauce is hot. Remove from heat; stir in mushrooms and onion.
5 Meanwhile, cook pasta in large saucepan of boiling water until tender; drain. Place pasta in large bowl with mushroom sauce, chorizo and basil; toss gently. Sprinkle with finely grated parmesan cheese and coarsely ground black pepper, if you like.

preparation time 10 minutes
cooking time 20 minutes **serves** 4
nutritional count per serving 66g total fat (30.4g saturated fat); 4397kJ (1028 cal); 69.7g carbohydrate; 32.5g protein; 5.8g fibre

chilli prawn linguine

500g linguine pasta
⅓ cup (80ml) olive oil
400g uncooked medium king prawns, peeled
3 fresh small red thai chillies, chopped finely
2 cloves garlic, crushed
½ cup finely chopped fresh flat-leaf parsley
2 teaspoons finely grated lemon rind

1 Cook pasta in large saucepan of boiling water until tender; drain.
2 Meanwhile, heat oil in large frying pan; cook prawns, chilli and garlic, stirring, until prawns are just cooked through. Remove from heat; stir in parsley and rind.
3 Combine pasta with prawn mixture in large bowl; toss gently.

preparation time 15 minutes
cooking time 15 minutes **serves** 4
nutritional count per serving 20.8g total fat (3g saturated fat); 2851kJ (682 cal); 85.5g carbohydrate; 34.7g protein; 4.8g fibre

chicken with red pesto pasta

4 chicken breast fillets (800g)
¼ cup (65g) bottled red pesto (*see note, below*)
375g linguine pasta
1 cup (70g) stale breadcrumbs
⅓ cup finely chopped fresh chives
2 teaspoons wholegrain mustard
½ cup (125ml) chicken stock

1 Preheat grill.
2 Coat chicken with half the pesto; cook under grill (or on grill plate or barbecue) until browned both sides and cooked through; cover to keep warm.
3 Meanwhile, cook pasta in large sauce pan of boiling water until tender; drain. Rinse under cold water; drain.
4 Heat oiled large saucepan; cook breadcrumbs, stirring, until browned. Stir in pasta, remaining pesto, chives, mustard and stock; cook, stirring, until hot.
5 Serve pasta with sliced chicken, and tomato wedges, if desired.

preparation time 10 minutes
cooking time 20 minutes **serves** 4
nutritional count per serving 14g total fat (3.2g saturated fat); 2926kJ (700 cal); 78.6g carbohydrate; 60.5g protein; 6.1g fibre

We used sun-dried capsicum pesto for this recipe, but any bottled 'red' pesto, such as tomato, could be used.

linguine with crab

300g fresh crab meat
1 clove garlic, crushed
2 fresh small red thai chillies, sliced thinly
½ cup (125ml) dry white wine
1 tablespoon finely grated lemon rind
375g linguine pasta
½ cup coarsely chopped fresh flat-leaf parsley
1 small red onion (100g), sliced thinly
⅓ cup (80ml) peanut oil

1 Cook crab, garlic and chilli in heated oiled large frying pan, stirring, until crab is just cooked.
2 Add wine and rind to pan; bring to the boil. Reduce heat; simmer, uncovered, until wine reduces by half.
3 Meanwhile, cook pasta in large saucepan of boiling water until tender; drain.
4 Combine pasta in large bowl with crab mixture and remaining ingredients; toss gently.

preparation time 10 minutes
cooking time 15 minutes **serves** 4
nutritional count per serving 19.7g total fat (3.6g saturated fat); 2324kJ (556 cal); 66.5g carbohydrate; 20.6g protein; 4g fibre

linguine with moroccan lamb sauce

2 teaspoons olive oil
1 small brown onion (80g), chopped finely
2 cloves garlic, crushed
500g lamb mince
1 teaspoon ground cumin
½ teaspoon cayenne pepper
½ teaspoon ground cinnamon
2 tablespoons tomato paste
2 x 415g cans crushed tomatoes
1 large green zucchini (150g), chopped coarsely
2 tablespoons finely chopped fresh mint
375g linguine or bucatini pasta

1 Heat oil in large saucepan; cook onion and garlic, stirring, until onion softens. Add lamb; cook, stirring, until changed in colour. Add spices; cook, stirring, until fragrant.
2 Add paste, undrained tomatoes and zucchini to pan; bring to the boil. Reduce heat; simmer, uncovered, about 15 minutes or until sauce thickens slightly. Stir in mint.
3 Meanwhile, cook pasta in large saucepan of boiling water until tender; drain. Serve pasta topped with sauce.

preparation time 10 minutes
cooking time 20 minutes **serves** 4
nutritional count per serving 16.2g total fat
(6.3g saturated fat); 2562kJ (613 cal); 73.4g carbohydrate;
38.9g protein; 7.3g fibre

macaroni

These small, hollow pasta tubes, which can be straight or bent (elbow macaroni), are made with semolina flour and water, but contain no eggs.

pastitsio

250g macaroni pasta
2 eggs, beaten lightly
¾ cup (60g) coarsely grated parmesan cheese
2 tablespoons stale breadcrumbs
meat sauce
1 tablespoon olive oil
2 medium brown onions (300g), chopped finely
750g beef mince
400g can chopped tomatoes
⅓ cup (95g) tomato paste
½ cup (125ml) beef stock
¼ cup (60ml) dry white wine
½ teaspoon ground cinnamon
1 egg, beaten lightly
cheese topping
90g butter
½ cup (75g) plain flour
3½ cups (875ml) milk
1 cup (80g) coarsely grated parmesan cheese
2 egg yolks

1 Preheat oven to 180°C/160°C fan-forced. Oil shallow 2.5-litre (10-cup) ovenproof dish.
2 Make meat sauce. Make cheese topping.
3 Cook pasta in large saucepan of boiling water until tender; drain. Combine warm pasta, egg and cheese in large bowl; mix well. Press pasta over base of dish; top with meat sauce, pour over cheese topping, smooth surface then sprinkle with breadcrumbs.
4 Bake, uncovered, in oven, about 1 hour or until browned lightly. Stand 10 minutes before serving.
meat sauce Heat oil in large saucepan; cook onion, stirring, until soft. Add beef; cook, stirring, until well browned. Stir in undrained tomatoes, paste, stock, wine and cinnamon; simmer, uncovered, until thick. Cool 10 minutes; stir in egg.
cheese topping Melt butter in medium saucepan, add flour; cook, stirring, until mixture thickens and bubbles. Gradually stir in milk; cook, stirring, until sauce boils and thickens. Remove from heat; stir in cheese. Cool 5 minutes; stir in egg yolks.

preparation time 30 minutes
cooking time 1 hour 45 minutes **serves** 6
nutritional count per serving 41.6g total fat (21.8g saturated fat); 3436kJ (822 cal); 54.4g carbohydrate; 54g protein; 3.8g fibre

beef, garlic & silver beet pasta bake

250g small macaroni pasta
2 teaspoons vegetable oil
4 cloves garlic, crushed
250g trimmed silver beet, sliced thinly
300g sour cream
5 cups bolognese sauce (*see note, below*)
½ cup (60g) coarsely grated cheddar cheese

1 Preheat oven to 200°C/180°C fan-forced.
2 Cook pasta in large saucepan of boiling water until tender; drain. Rinse under cold water; drain.
3 Meanwhile, heat oil in large frying pan; cook garlic, stirring, 1 minute. Add silver beet; cook, stirring, until wilted. Stir in pasta and sour cream.
4 Spread half the bolognese sauce into shallow 3-litre (12-cup) baking dish. Layer with half the silver beet mixture; top with remaining sauce then remaining silver beet mixture. Sprinkle over cheese.
5 Bake, uncovered, in oven, about 20 minutes or until browned and heated through.

preparation time 10 minutes
cooking time 40 minutes **serves** 6
nutritional count per serving 38.2g total fat (20.5g saturated fat); 2654kJ (635 cal); 38.7g carbohydrate; 31.7g protein; 6g fibre

The bolognese sauce used for this recipe is from the double amount made for the recipe on page 88. You will need to make that sauce recipe first, to get the amount of bolognese sauce required for this recipe. Freeze leftover sauce for up to three months.

macaroni cheese

1 cup (180g) macaroni pasta
30g butter
2 tablespoons plain flour
2 teaspoons mustard powder
1½ cups (375ml) milk
¾ cup (90g) grated cheddar cheese
2 hard-boiled eggs, quartered
½ cup (60g) frozen peas, thawed
2 tablespoons finely chopped fresh flat-leaf parsley

1 Cook pasta in large saucepan of boiling water until tender; drain.
2 Meanwhile, melt butter in large saucepan, add flour and mustard; cook, stirring constantly, over medium heat, about 2 minutes or until mixture thickens and bubbles, do not allow mixture to brown. Remove from heat; gradually stir in milk. Return to medium heat; stir until sauce boils and thickens slightly. Add cheese; stir until melted.
3 Gently stir pasta, egg, peas and parsley into sauce; serve immediately.

preparation time 15 minutes
cooking time 40 minutes **serves** 4
nutritional count per serving 21.7g total fat
(12.3g saturated fat); 1843kJ (441 cal); 40.6g carbohydrate; 19.5g protein; 2.7g fibre

If you prefer, instead of serving in step 3, place the mixture into a heatproof dish; sprinkle with a little extra cheese then place under a hot grill for a few minutes until lightly browned. Or, place the mixture in an ovenproof dish; bake, uncovered, in a moderate oven for about 20 minutes or until browned lightly and heated through.

spicy sausage pasta bake

375g macaroni pasta
6 thick spicy lamb sausages (900g)
1 medium brown onion (150g), chopped coarsely
1 small eggplant (230g), chopped coarsely
2 medium red capsicums (400g), chopped coarsely
3 small green zucchini (270g), chopped coarsely
700g bottled tomato pasta sauce
½ cup coarsely chopped fresh basil
2 cups (200g) pizza cheese

1 Preheat oven to 180°C/160°C fan-forced.
2 Cook pasta in large saucepan of boiling water until tender; drain.
3 Meanwhile, cook sausages in heated oiled large frying pan until just cooked through. Drain on absorbent paper.
4 Cook onion, eggplant, capsicum and zucchini in same pan, stirring, until just tender.
5 Cut sausages into 2cm slices; add to vegetables in pan with sauce and basil, stir to combine.
6 Combine pasta and sausage mixture in deep 3-litre (12-cup) casserole dish; sprinkle with cheese. Bake, uncovered, in oven about 20 minutes or until browned lightly.

preparation time 15 minutes
cooking time 35 minutes **serves** 6
nutritional count per serving 36.3g total fat (16.5g saturated fat); 3453kJ (826 cal); 67.7g carbohydrate; 57.6g protein; 7.5g fibre

macaroni with beef sausages

400g thin beef sausages
600ml bottled tomato pasta sauce
4 stalks celery (600g), trimmed, chopped coarsely
1 medium green capsicum (200g), chopped coarsely
250g elbow macaroni pasta
2 tablespoons finely chopped fresh basil
1 cup (100g) grated mozzarella

1 Cook sausages, in batches, in heated oiled large frying pan until browned all over and cooked through; drain on absorbent paper. Cut sausages into 1cm slices.
2 Place sauce in same cleaned pan; bring to the boil. Add sausage, celery and capsicum; cook, stirring occasionally, about 5 minutes or until vegetables are just tender.
3 Meanwhile, cook pasta in large saucepan of boiling water until tender; drain.
4 Combine pasta, basil and cheese in pan with sausage and tomato sauce; toss gently.

preparation time 10 minutes
cooking time 20 minutes **serves** 4
nutritional count per serving 33g total fat (16g saturated fat); 2863kJ (685 cal); 63.4g carbohydrate; 28.8g protein; 10g fibre

Try making this recipe with some of the more exotic sausages so readily available these days (one variety with fennel and chilli is especially delicious when cooked in tomato sauce).

pappardelle

Pappardelle is the widest ribbon pasta available;
any long pasta such as fettuccine or tagliatelle can
be substituted in these recipes.

pappardelle with chilli & semi-dried tomato sauce

2 medium brown onions (300g), chopped coarsely
2 cloves garlic, quartered
1 cup (150g) semi-dried tomatoes in oil, drained
¼ cup (70g) tomato paste
2 fresh small red thai chillies, chopped finely
2 cups (500ml) beef stock (*see note, below*)
375g pappardelle pasta
¼ cup coarsely chopped fresh flat-leaf parsley

1   Blend or process onion, garlic, tomatoes, paste and
chilli until mixture forms a paste.
2   Heat oiled large frying pan; cook tomato mixture,
stirring, 10 minutes. Stir in stock; bring to the boil. Reduce
heat; simmer sauce, uncovered, about 10 minutes or
until thickened slightly.
3   Meanwhile, cook pasta in large saucepan of boiling
water until tender; drain.
4   Gently toss pasta through sauce; sprinkle with parsley.

preparation time 15 minutes
cooking time 25 minutes **serves** 6
nutritional count per serving 2.9g total fat
(0.4g saturated fat); 1313kJ (314 cal); 55.7g carbohydrate;
11.9g protein; 7g fibre

To make this a meal suitable for vegetarians,
substitute vegetable stock for the beef stock.

pappardelle with roasted mushrooms & tomato

200g flat mushrooms, quartered
200g button mushrooms
200g swiss brown mushrooms
250g cherry tomatoes
½ cup (125ml) chicken stock (*see note, below*)
2 teaspoons garlic salt
375g pappardelle or fettuccine pasta
¼ cup torn fresh basil leaves
¼ cup (20g) coarsely grated parmesan cheese

1 Preheat oven to 220°C/200°C fan-forced.
2 Combine mushrooms, tomatoes and stock in baking dish; sprinkle with salt. Bake, uncovered, about 20 minutes or until mushrooms are tender and tomatoes softened.
3 Meanwhile, cook pasta in large pan of boiling water until just tender; drain.
4 Gently toss mushroom mixture through pasta; sprinkle with basil and cheese.

preparation time 10 minutes
cooking time 20 minutes **serves** 4
nutritional count per serving 3.3g total fat (1.3g saturated fat); 1618kJ (387 cal); 66g carbohydrate; 18.5g protein; 7.9g fibre

To make this a meal suitable for vegetarians, substitute vegetable stock for the chicken stock.

pappardelle with chicken & creamy mushroom sauce

2 tablespoons olive oil
1 clove garlic, crushed
1 small brown onion (80g), chopped finely
250g swiss brown mushrooms, sliced thinly
1 cup (250ml) cream
2 teaspoons finely chopped fresh rosemary
50g butter, chopped
500g pappardelle pasta
200g cooked chicken, shredded thinly
½ cup (55g) coarsely chopped walnuts, roasted
¾ cup (60g) grated parmesan cheese
¼ cup coarsely chopped fresh flat-leaf parsley

1 Heat oil in large frying pan; cook garlic and onion, stirring, until onion softens. Add mushroom; cook, stirring, until tender.
2 Add cream and rosemary to pan. Bring to the boil; reduce heat. Simmer, uncovered, about 3 minutes or until sauce thickens; stir in butter.
3 Meanwhile, cook pasta in large saucepan of boiling water until tender; drain, return pasta to pan.
4 Add hot cream sauce to hot pasta with chicken, nuts, half the cheese and parsley; toss gently.
5 Serve immediately, topped with remaining cheese.

preparation time 15 minutes
cooking time 12 minutes **serves** 6
nutritional count per serving 43.5g total fat (20.6g saturated fat); 3085kJ (738 cal); 59.4g carbohydrate; 25g protein; 5.5g fibre

clear prawn & crushed noodle soup

500g uncooked medium king prawns
150g pappardelle or fettuccine pasta, broken roughly
1.25 litres (5 cups) chicken stock
2 cups (500ml) water
20g piece fresh galangal, chopped finely
4cm piece fresh ginger (20g), chopped finely
4 kaffir lime leaves
10cm stick fresh lemon grass (20g), finely chopped
⅓ cup (80ml) lemon juice
¼ cup (60ml) fish sauce
1 tablespoon sambal oelek
1 fresh small red thai chilli, sliced thinly
¼ cup coarsely chopped fresh coriander

1 Shell and devein prawns, leaving tails intact.
2 Cook pasta in large saucepan of boiling water until tender; drain.
3 Meanwhile, combine stock, the water, galangal, ginger, lime leaves and lemon grass in large saucepan; bring to the boil. Boil, uncovered, about 5 minutes or until reduced by a quarter. Add juice, sauce, sambal and prawns, reduce heat; cook, uncovered, until prawns just change in colour. Remove from heat; discard lime leaves, add chilli and coriander.
4 Divide pasta and prawn mixture among serving bowls; ladle soup over the top.

preparation time 10 minutes
cooking time 15 minutes **serves** 4
nutritional count per serving 2.3g total fat
(0.8g saturated fat); 986kJ (236 cal); 30.5g carbohydrate; 22.1g protein; 1.8g fibre

chicken liver sauce with pappardelle

500g chicken livers, trimmed
½ cup (50g) packaged breadcrumbs
¼ cup (60ml) olive oil
1 medium brown onion (150g), chopped coarsely
4 medium tomatoes (600g), chopped coarsely
½ cup (125ml) chicken stock
¼ cup (60ml) balsamic vinegar
¼ cup (60ml) dry red wine
2 tablespoons coarsely chopped fresh rosemary
375g pappardelle pasta or curly lasagne sliced thickly

1 Halve livers; toss in breadcrumbs, shake off excess. Heat half of the oil in large frying pan; cook liver over high heat, in batches, until browned and cooked (*see note, below*).
2 Heat remaining oil in same pan; cook onion, stirring, until soft. Add tomato; cook, stirring, until tomato is pulpy. Add stock, vinegar, wine and rosemary to the pan; cook, stirring, until sauce thickens slightly.
3 Meanwhile, cook pasta in large saucepan of boiling water until tender; drain.
4 Stir pasta and liver into tomato sauce; toss gently.

preparation time 10 minutes
cooking time 20 minutes **serves** 4
nutritional count per serving 20.3g total fat (3.9g saturated fat); 2801kJ (670 cal); 78.6g carbohydrate; 37.1g protein; 5.9g fibre

Be sure not to overcook the chicken livers or they will be dry and unappealing.

penne

This cylinder shaped pasta, named after a pen or quill because of its shape, can be smooth (lisce) or ridged (rigate). It is a perennial favourite as the hollow centre allows it to hold more sauce.

pepper-crusted lamb fillet with penne in red capsicum sauce

3 medium red capsicums (600g)
600g lamb fillets
1 tablespoon cracked black pepper
1 tablespoon olive oil
1 medium brown onion (150g), chopped finely
2 cloves garlic, crushed
300ml cream
375g penne pasta
⅔ cup coarsely chopped fresh basil

1 Quarter capsicums; discard seeds and membranes. Roast, skin-side up, under very hot grill until skin blisters and blackens. Cover capsicum pieces in plastic or paper for 5 minutes; peel away skin then chop coarsely.
2 Combine lamb and pepper in medium bowl; cook lamb, in batches, in heated oiled large frying pan until browned all over and cooked as desired. Cover lamb; stand 5 minutes then slice thinly.
3 Heat oil in same pan; cook onion and garlic, stirring, until onion softens. Add cream; bring to the boil. Remove from heat; blend or process cream mixture with capsicum until mixture is smooth.
4 Meanwhile, cook pasta in large saucepan of boiling water until tender; drain.
5 Place pasta in large bowl with lamb, sauce and basil; toss gently.

preparation time 10 minutes
cooking time 25 minutes **serves** 4
nutritional count per serving 51.9g total fat (28.5g saturated fat); 3946kJ (944 cal); 73.3g carbohydrate; 46.3g protein; 6.1g fibre

penne, parmesan & asparagus hollandaise

¼ cup (60ml) white vinegar
1 tablespoon coarsely chopped fresh tarragon
8 whole black peppercorns
4 egg yolks
250g cold unsalted butter, chopped
1 tablespoon lemon juice
375g penne pasta
1kg asparagus, trimmed, chopped coarsely
⅓ cup (25g) grated parmesan cheese

1 Combine vinegar, tarragon and peppercorns in small saucepan; bring to the boil. Reduce heat; simmer, uncovered, until mixture reduces to about 1 tablespoon. Strain vinegar mixture into large heatproof bowl; discard tarragon and peppercorns. Place bowl over large saucepan of simmering water; whisk in egg yolks until mixture is light and fluffy (do not allow water to touch base of bowl). Gradually add butter, whisking continuously between additions, until hollandaise sauce thickens; stir in juice.
2 Cook pasta in large saucepan of boiling water until tender; drain.
3 Meanwhile, boil, steam or microwave asparagus until just tender; drain.
4 Place pasta, asparagus, cheese and hollandaise sauce in large bowl; toss gently.

preparation time 15 minutes
cooking time 15 minutes **serves** 4
nutritional count per serving 60.1g total fat (36.9g saturated fat); 3754kJ (898 cal); 66.9g carbohydrate; 28.7g protein; 5.6g fibre

baked penne with peas, mushrooms & leek

400g penne pasta
2 tablespoons vegetable oil
50g butter
1 clove garlic, crushed
2 small leeks (400g), sliced thinly
300g button mushrooms, sliced thinly
⅓ cup finely chopped fresh chives
2 cups (240g) frozen peas, thawed
béchamel sauce
100g butter
⅔ cup (100g) plain flour
1.25 litres (5 cups) hot milk
2½ cups (300g) coarsely grated cheddar cheese

1 Cook pasta in large saucepan of boiling water until tender; drain.
2 Meanwhile, make béchamel sauce.
3 Preheat oven to 180°C/160°C fan-forced.
4 Heat oil and butter in medium frying pan; cook garlic, leek and mushrooms, stirring, until leek softens.
5 Combine pasta and leek mixture in large bowl with chives and peas. Reserve ⅔ cup béchamel sauce for top. Stir remaining sauce into leek mixture. Spoon leek mixture into 3.75-litre (15-cup) ovenproof dish; spread with reserved béchamel sauce.
6 Bake, uncovered, in oven about 40 minutes or until browned lightly.
béchamel sauce Melt butter in medium saucepan, add flour; cook, stirring, until mixture thickens and bubbles. Gradually stir in milk; stir until sauce boils and thickens. Remove from heat; stir in cheese.

preparation time 15 minutes
cooking time 1 hour 10 minutes **serves** 6
nutritional count per serving 53.1g total fat (30.6g saturated fat); 3825kJ (915 cal); 71.9g carbohydrate; 34.2g protein; 7.7g fibre

penne arrabiata

1 tablespoon olive oil
2 medium brown onions (300g), chopped finely
5 cloves garlic, crushed
3 fresh small red thai chillies, chopped finely
2⅓ cups (600ml) bottled tomato pasta sauce
2 teaspoons balsamic vinegar
375g penne pasta
¼ cup (20g) finely grated parmesan cheese

1 Heat oil in large saucepan; cook onion, garlic and chilli, stirring, until onion softens. Add sauce and vinegar; bring to the boil. Reduce heat; simmer, uncovered, about 5 minutes or until sauce thickens slightly.
2 Meanwhile, cook pasta in large saucepan of boiling water, uncovered, until just tender; drain. Combine pasta with sauce; sprinkle with cheese.

preparation time 10 minutes
cooking time 15 minutes **serves** 4
nutritional count per serving 8.6g total fat (2.1g saturated fat); 2082kJ (498 cal); 84.2g carbohydrate; 16.1g protein; 7.8g fibre

Place leftover pasta and sauce in an oiled ovenproof dish, cover with mozzarella and bake in a moderate oven until heated through and cheese bubbles.

penne primavera

375g penne pasta
1 tablespoon olive oil
1 large brown onion (200g), chopped finely
2 cloves garlic, crushed
4 baby carrots (50g), chopped finely
150g green beans, chopped finely
100g snow peas, trimmed, halved
250g asparagus, chopped coarsely
1 tablespoon fresh oregano leaves
2 teaspoons fresh thyme leaves
400g can diced tomatoes
1¼ cups (100g) shaved parmesan cheese

1 Cook pasta in large saucepan of boiling water until tender; drain.
2 Meanwhile, heat oil in large frying pan. Cook onion, stirring occasionally, over low heat, until very soft but not browned. Add garlic and carrot; cook 1 minute.
3 Stir in beans; cook until changed in colour. Stir in snow peas and asparagus; cook until changed in colour. Add herbs and tomato; bring to the boil. Reduce heat; simmer until heated through and thickened slightly.
4 Toss pasta through hot sauce; serve with cheese.

preparation time 25 minutes
cooking time 25 minutes **serves** 4
nutritional count per serving 14.5g total fat (6.1g saturated fat); 2307kJ (552 cal); 75.1g carbohydrate; 25.8g protein; 7.1g fibre

lamb & capsicum pasta

3 large red capsicums (1kg), quartered
500g lamb fillets
2 tablespoons olive oil
2 teaspoons ground cumin
2 x 415g cans tomato puree
½ cup (75g) drained semi-dried tomatoes in oil,
    chopped coarsely
375g penne pasta
¼ cup finely shredded fresh basil

1 Roast capsicum, skin-side up, under very hot grill until skin blisters and blackens. Cover in plastic or paper for 5 minutes; peel away skin then chop coarsely.
2 Combine lamb, oil and cumin in bowl; cook lamb, in batches, in heated oiled large frying pan until cooked. Stand 5 minutes, then cut into thin slices.
3 Bring puree, tomato and capsicum to the boil in heated large frying pan. Simmer, uncovered, about 5 minutes or until sauce thickens slightly.
4 Cook pasta in large saucepan of boiling water until tender; drain. Place pasta in large bowl with lamb, tomato sauce and basil; toss gently.

preparation time 10 minutes
cooking time 15 minutes **serves** 4
nutritional count per serving 16.7g total fat
(3.6g saturated fat); 2989kJ (715 cal); 89.9g carbohydrate;
44.5g protein; 12.2g fibre

penne chilli con carne

375g penne pasta
1 tablespoon peanut oil
1 large brown onion (200g), sliced thinly
2 cloves garlic, crushed
2 fresh small red thai chillies, chopped coarsely
1 teaspoon ground cumin
1 teaspoon ground coriander
350g yellow cherry tomatoes, halved
500g thinly sliced cooked roast beef
420g can kidney beans, rinsed, drained
2⅓ cups (600g) bottled tomato pasta sauce
⅓ cup loosely packed fresh coriander leaves

1 Cook pasta in large saucepan of boiling water until tender; drain.
2 Meanwhile, heat oil in large saucepan; cook onion, garlic, chilli and ground spices, stirring, until onion softens. Add tomato; cook, stirring, until tomato is just soft. Add beef, beans and sauce; bring to the boil. Simmer, uncovered, until sauce thickens slightly.
3 Add pasta to pan; toss gently over heat until hot. Stir in fresh coriander.

preparation time 8 minutes
cooking time 20 minutes **serves** 4
nutritional count per serving 12.9g total fat
(3.9g saturated fat); 3022kJ (723 cal); 93.1g carbohydrate;
50.8g protein; 12.8g fibre

ravioli & tortellini

Ravioli are little pillows of pasta stuffed with a variety of delicious fillings including meat, fish, cheese and vegetables. Tortellini are very similar, but are formed into a ring shape.

ravioli with asian greens

1 tablespoon sesame oil
4 green onions, chopped finely
4cm piece fresh ginger (20g), grated
4 cloves garlic, crushed
450g chicken mince
2 tablespoons soy sauce
½ teaspoon five-spice powder
100g wombok, sliced thinly
¼ cup coarsely chopped fresh coriander
40 wonton wrappers
1½ cups (375ml) chicken stock
1½ cups (375ml) water
2 fresh small red thai chillies, chopped finely
2 tablespoons soy sauce, extra
1 tablespoon char siu sauce
¼ cup (60ml) chinese cooking wine
500g baby buk choy, quartered lengthways
150g snow peas, trimmed, halved

1 Heat oil in wok; stir-fry onion, ginger and garlic until onion softens. Add mince; stir-fry until mince changes colour. Add soy sauce, five-spice and wombok; stir-fry until wombok is tender. Stir in coriander; cool 10 minutes.
2 Place 1 level tablespoon of the mince mixture in centre of one wrapper; brush around edges with water. Top with another wrapper; press edges together to seal. Repeat with remaining mince mixture and wrappers.
3 Add stock, the water, chilli, extra soy sauce, char siu sauce and cooking wine to same cleaned wok; bring to the boil. Add pasta to wok; boil until pasta floats to the top. Using slotted spoon, remove pasta from stock mixture; cover to keep warm.
4 Cook buk choy and snow peas in stock mixture until vegetables are tender.
5 Divide pasta and vegetables among serving bowls; ladle over stock mixture.

preparation time 40 minutes
cooking time 30 minutes **serves** 4
nutritional count per serving 15.8g total fat (3.8g saturated fat); 2161kJ (517 cal); 52.9g carbohydrate; 35.9g protein; 4.3g fibre

cheese & spinach tortellini with gorgonzola sauce

30g butter
2 tablespoons plain flour
1 cup (250ml) milk
¾ cup (180ml) cream
100g gorgonzola cheese, chopped coarsely
750g packaged cheese and spinach tortellini
¼ cup loosely packed fresh flat-leaf parsley leaves

1 Melt butter in medium saucepan, add flour; cook, stirring, about 2 minutes or until mixture bubbles and thickens. Gradually stir in milk and cream; bring to the boil. Reduce heat; simmer, uncovered, until sauce boils and thickens. Remove from heat; stir in cheese.
2 Meanwhile, cook pasta in large saucepan of boiling water until pasta floats to the top; drain.
3 Combine pasta with sauce; sprinkle with parsley.

preparation time 5 minutes
cooking time 15 minutes **serves** 4
nutritional count per serving 58.5g total fat (37.4g saturated fat); 3741kJ (895 cal); 56.2g carbohydrate; 34g protein; 5.8g fibre

Ravioli or gnocchi can be substituted for the tortellini. It's best to choose a ricotta-and-spinach-filled tortellini (or even just a plain ricotta-filled version) when making this sauce, as it doesn't marry overly well with meat-filled pastas.

ricotta & capsicum ravioli with rocket dressing

3 large red capsicums (1kg)
2 green onions, chopped finely
1 clove garlic, crushed
2½ cups (600g) ricotta cheese
72 wonton wrappers
300g baby rocket leaves
½ cup (125ml) olive oil
2 tablespoons lemon juice
2 tablespoons balsamic vinegar
2 teaspoons white sugar
1 clove garlic, quartered, extra
¼ cup (20g) shaved parmesan cheese

1 Quarter capsicums; discard seeds and membranes. Roast, skin-side up, under very hot grill until skin blisters and blackens. Cover capsicum pieces in plastic or paper for 5 minutes; peel away skin then chop finely.
2 Combine capsicum, onion, garlic and ricotta in bowl.
3 Place level tablespoons of the capsicum filling in the centre of 36 wonton wrappers; brush edges lightly with a little water. Top each with remaining wonton wrappers; press edges together to seal.
4 Reserve approximately a fifth of the rocket. Process remaining rocket, oil, juice, vinegar, sugar and extra garlic until pureed. Strain into medium jug; discard pulp.
5 Cook pasta in large saucepan of boiling water until pasta floats to the top; drain. Serve pasta drizzled with rocket dressing; top with cheese and reserved rocket.

preparation time 40 minutes
cooking time 30 minutes **serves** 6
nutritional count per serving 33.1g total fat (10.9g saturated fat); 1889kJ (452 cal); 12.2g carbohydrate; 25.9g protein; 2.6g fibre

scallop mousse ravioli in star anise broth

80g angel hair pasta

300g scallops, roe removed

2 tablespoons coarsely chopped fresh coriander

2 teaspoons finely chopped fresh lemon grass

1cm piece fresh ginger (5g), grated

2 tablespoons fish sauce

2 egg whites

1 litre (4 cups) chicken stock

1½ cups (375ml) fish stock

2 star anise

40 wonton wrappers

1 green onion

1 tablespoon drained sliced pink pickled ginger

1 fresh small red thai chilli, sliced finely

⅓ cup firmly packed coriander leaves

1 Cook pasta in medium saucepan of boiling water until tender; drain. Using kitchen scissors, chop into random lengths; reserve.

2 Blend or process scallops, chopped coriander, lemon grass, fresh ginger, sauce and egg whites until mixture forms a smooth paste.

3 Bring stocks and star anise to the boil in large saucepan. Reduce heat; simmer, covered, while making ravioli.

4 Place level tablespoons of scallop mixture in the centre of 20 wonton wrappers; brush edges lightly with a little water. Top each with remaining wonton wrappers; press edges together to seal ravioli.

5 Trim onion; cut crossways into quarters, cut each quarter lengthways into thin strips. Cut pickled ginger into thin strips. Divide onion, pickled ginger, noodles, chilli and coriander leaves among soup bowls.

6 Cook ravioli, in batches, in large saucepan of boiling water until ravioli floats to the top; drain. Divide among bowls. Discard star anise from hot broth; ladle over ravioli.

preparation time 40 minutes
cooking time 20 minutes **serves** 4
nutritional count per serving 3g total fat (1g saturated fat); 898kJ (215 cal); 19.6g carbohydrate; 26.4g protein; 1.1g fibre

ravioli with fennel & leek

80g butter
2 tablespoons olive oil
1 large fennel bulb (550g), trimmed, sliced thinly
1 large leek (500g), chopped finely
⅓ cup (80ml) dry white wine
1 tablespoon white sugar
300g beef mince
270g packet wonton wrappers
1 egg, beaten lightly
2 tablespoons lemon juice
1 clove garlic, crushed
1 tablespoon finely chopped fresh chives

1 Heat a quarter of the butter with half of the oil in large frying pan; cook fennel and leek, stirring, 5 minutes. Stir in wine and sugar; bring to the boil. Reduce heat; simmer, covered, stirring occasionally, about 20 minutes or until liquid is absorbed and vegetables are caramelised.
2 Meanwhile, combine mince with remaining oil in medium bowl.
3 Place a heaped teaspoon of mince mixture in centre of one wonton wrapper, brush edges with a little egg; top with another wrapper, press edges together to seal. Repeat with remaining mince mixture, wrappers and egg.
4 Cook pasta, in batches, in large saucepan of boiling water until pasta floats to the top and mince is cooked through; drain. Toss pasta in large bowl with remaining chopped butter, juice and garlic.
5 Divide pasta among serving bowls; top with caramelised fennel and leek; sprinkle with chives.

preparation time 30 minutes
cooking time 25 minutes **serves** 4
nutritional count per serving 33.2g total fat (14.9g saturated fat); 1960kJ (469 cal); 11.5g carbohydrate; 26.7g protein; 4.2g fibre

chicken ravioli with tarragon sauce

750g chicken mince
2 green onions, sliced thinly
2 teaspoons finely grated lemon rind
56 gow gee wrappers
1 egg, beaten lightly
2 teaspoons olive oil
1 medium brown onion (150g), chopped finely
2 cloves garlic, crushed
½ cup (125ml) dry white wine
1 tablespoon dijon mustard
2⅓ cups (580ml) cream
2 tablespoons finely shredded fresh tarragon

1 Combine chicken, green onion and rind in bowl.
2 Brush one wrapper at a time with egg. Place a rounded teaspoon of the chicken mixture in centre of wrapper. Fold over to enclose filling; press edge to seal. Repeat to make a total of 56 ravioli. Place ravioli, in single layer, on tray. Cover; refrigerate 30 minutes.
3 Heat oil in medium saucepan; cook brown onion and garlic, stirring, until onion is just browned. Add wine; cook, stirring, about 5 minutes or until wine reduces by half. Stir in mustard and cream; cook sauce, stirring, until mixture just boils.
4 Meanwhile, cook pasta in large saucepan of boiling water until pasta floats to the top; drain. Add pasta and tarragon to cream sauce. Toss gently until pasta is warmed through.

preparation time 25 minutes (plus refrigeration time)
cooking time 30 minutes **serves** 8
nutritional count per serving 41.5g total fat (23.5g saturated fat); 2119kJ (507 cal); 4.9g carbohydrate; 26.9g protein; 0.5g fibre

rigatoni

Rigatoni, a ridged, tube-shaped pasta, is ideal for 'pasta al forno' (baked dishes) because it is wide and the hearty fillings cling to the indentations around the edges.

chicken, mushroom & asparagus creamy pasta bake

375g rigatoni pasta
60g butter
600g chicken breast fillets, cut into 1cm pieces
100g button mushrooms, sliced thinly
2 tablespoons plain flour
2 cups (500ml) milk
½ cup (40g) coarsely grated pecorino cheese
1¼ cups (150g) coarsely grated cheddar cheese
170g asparagus, trimmed, chopped coarsely
¼ cup coarsely chopped fresh flat-leaf parsley

1 Preheat oven to 200°C/180°C fan-forced.
2 Cook pasta in large saucepan of boiling water until tender; drain.
3 Meanwhile, heat a third of the butter in large frying pan; cook chicken, in batches, until browned and cooked through.
4 Heat remaining butter in same pan; cook mushrooms, stirring, until tender. Add flour; cook, stirring, 1 minute. Gradually add milk, stirring over medium heat until mixture boils and thickens. Stir in chicken, ¼ cup of the pecorino, ¾ cup of the cheddar and the asparagus.
5 Combine chicken mixture and drained pasta in 2.5-litre (10-cup) ovenproof dish; sprinkle with remaining cheeses. Cook, uncovered, in oven about 15 minutes or until top browns lightly. Serve pasta bake sprinkled with parsley.

preparation time 20 minutes
cooking time 30 minutes **serves** 4
nutritional count per serving 37.3g total fat (22.3g saturated fat); 3775kJ (903 cal); 75.2g carbohydrate; 64g protein; 4.8g fibre

salmon & pea pasta bake

375g rigatoni pasta
40g butter
2 tablespoons plain flour
2 cups (500ml) milk
1½ cups (180g) frozen peas
½ cup (40g) coarsely grated parmesan cheese
1¼ cups (150g) coarsely grated cheddar cheese
415g can pink salmon, drained, skin and
    bones removed

1 Preheat oven to 200°C/180°C fan-forced.
2 Cook pasta in large saucepan of boiling water until tender; drain.
3 Meanwhile, melt butter in medium saucepan, add flour; cook, stirring, until mixture thickens and bubbles. Gradually add milk, stirring over medium heat until sauce boils and thickens. Stir in peas, ¼ cup parmesan and ¾ cup cheddar cheese.
4 Combine sauce mixture with pasta and salmon in shallow 2.5-litre (10-cup) oiled ovenproof dish; sprinkle with remaining combined cheeses. Bake, uncovered, in oven, about 20 minutes or until browned lightly.

preparation time 15 minutes
cooking time 35 minutes **serves** 6
nutritional count per serving 23.8g total fat
(13.7g saturated fat); 2345kJ (561 cal);
51.2g carbohydrate; 33.1g protein; 3.9g fibre

rigatoni with brie, walnut & mushroom sauce

1 tablespoon olive oil
1 clove garlic, crushed
200g button mushrooms, halved
½ cup (125ml) dry white wine
2 tablespoons wholegrain mustard
600ml cream
375g rigatoni pasta
200g brie cheese, chopped coarsely
1 cup (100g) walnuts, roasted, chopped coarsely
¼ cup coarsely chopped fresh chives

1 Heat oil in large frying pan; cook garlic and mushrooms, stirring, until mushrooms are just tender. Add wine; boil, uncovered, until wine reduces by half.
2 Add mustard and cream to mushroom mixture; cook, stirring, until sauce thickens slightly.
3 Meanwhile, cook pasta in large saucepan of boiling water until tender; drain.
4 Place pasta, cheese, nuts, chives and sauce in large bowl; toss gently.

preparation time 5 minutes
cooking time 20 minutes **serves** 4
nutritional count per serving 69.9g total fat
(32.4g saturated fat); 4466kJ (1067 cal); 72g carbohydrate;
30.6g protein; 6.4g fibre

rigatoni with cauliflower & broccoli

375g rigatoni pasta
⅓ cup (80ml) extra virgin olive oil
5 cloves garlic, chopped coarsely
1½ cups (105g) stale breadcrumbs
350g cauliflower florets
350g broccoli florets
⅓ cup (80ml) lemon juice
1 cup coarsely chopped fresh flat-leaf parsley
½ cup (40g) toasted flaked almonds

1 Cook pasta in large saucepan of boiling water until just tender; drain.
2 Meanwhile, heat 2 tablespoons of the oil in large frying pan; cook garlic and breadcrumbs, stirring, until browned lightly. Place in large serving bowl.
3 Heat remaining oil in same pan; cook cauliflower and broccoli, in batches, stirring, until almost tender. Add vegetables, pasta, juice, parsley and nuts to large bowl with breadcrumb mixture; toss to combine.

preparation time 25 minutes
cooking time 15 minutes **serves** 4
nutritional count per serving 26.3g total fat (3.3g saturated fat); 2897kJ (693 cal); 85g carbohydrate; 22.9g protein; 11.6g fibre

rigatoni with fetta & red capsicum sauce

375g rigatoni pasta
2 medium tomatoes (300g), seeded, sliced
1 small red onion (100g), sliced thinly
¼ cup fresh flat-leaf parsley leaves
90g low-fat fetta cheese, crumbled
red capsicum sauce
1 small red capsicum (150g), quartered
1 clove garlic, crushed
1 teaspoon coarsely chopped fresh thyme
1 tablespoon red wine vinegar
1 tablespoon lemon juice
⅓ cup (80ml) vegetable stock

1 Make red capsicum sauce.
2 Cook pasta in large saucepan of boiling water until tender; drain. Toss hot pasta with tomato, onion, parsley and capsicum sauce in large bowl; sprinkle with cheese.
red capsicum sauce Roast capsicum, skin-side up, under very hot grill until skin blackens. Cover with plastic wrap for 5 minutes; peel away skin then chop coarsely. Blend with remaining ingredients until smooth. Sieve.

preparation time 25 minutes
cooking time 15 minutes **serves** 4
nutritional count per serving 4.6g total fat (2.3g saturated fat); 1680kJ (402 cal); 68.4g carbohydrate; 18.3g protein; 5g fibre

rigatoni with tomato & red wine sauce

30g butter
1 medium brown onion (150g), chopped finely
1 clove garlic, crushed
410g can crushed tomatoes
¼ cup (60ml) dry red wine
¼ cup (60ml) water
2 teaspoons tomato paste
1 chicken stock cube (*see note, below*)
1 teaspoon cornflour
1 tablespoon water, extra
1 teaspoon white sugar
2 teaspoons finely chopped fresh basil
1 tablespoon finely chopped fresh flat-leaf parsley
375g rigatoni pasta

1 Melt butter in large frying pan; cook onion and garlic, stirring, over medium heat until onion is soft. Add undrained tomatoes, wine, the water, paste and crumbled stock cube; bring to the boil. Reduce heat; simmer, uncovered, 10 minutes.
2 Stir blended cornflour and the extra water into tomato mixture; stir constantly over high heat until mixture boils and thickens. Stir in sugar and herbs.
3 Meanwhile, cook pasta in large saucepan of boiling water until tender; drain.
4 Serve sauce spooned over pasta.

preparation time 10 minutes
cooking time 20 minutes **serves** 4
nutritional count per serving 7.5g total fat
(4.3g saturated fat); 1781kJ (426 cal); 71.4g carbohydrate;
12.2g protein; 5.1g fibre

For a recipe suitable for vegetarians, use a vegetable stock cube instead of the chicken stock cube.

rigatoni with eggplant sauce

¼ cup (60ml) olive oil
1 medium onion (150g), chopped finely
2 stalks celery (300g), trimmed, chopped finely
1 clove garlic, crushed
2 tablespoons brandy (optional)
1 medium eggplant (300g), sliced thinly
2⅓ cups (600g) bottled tomato pasta sauce
½ cup (140g) tomato paste
½ cup (125ml) water
375g rigatoni pasta
¼ cup (20g) finely grated parmesan cheese

1 Heat oil in large saucepan; cook onion, celery and garlic, stirring, until onion softens. Add brandy; cook, stirring, until brandy evaporates. Add eggplant; cook, stirring, until tender.
2 Add sauce, paste and the water to pan; bring to the boil. Reduce heat; simmer, uncovered, about 10 minutes or until sauce thickens slightly.
3 Meanwhile, cook pasta in large saucepan of boiling water until tender; drain.
4 Place pasta in large bowl with half the eggplant sauce; toss gently. Divide pasta among serving plates; top with remaining sauce, sprinkle over cheese.

preparation time 10 minutes
cooking time 20 minutes **serves** 4
nutritional count per serving 17g total fat (3.1g saturated fat); 2934kJ (702 cal); 109g carbohydrate; 16g protein; 10.6g fibre

risoni

Risoni, a small, rice-shaped pasta very similar to orzo, is often used as an ingredient in soups and salads rather than served on its own.

seafood risoni paella

12 uncooked medium king prawns (540g)
250g small mussels
300g firm white fish fillets
2 tablespoons olive oil
1 small brown onion (80g), chopped finely
4 cloves garlic, crushed
500g risoni pasta
pinch saffron threads
1 cup (250ml) dry white wine
6 small tomatoes (540g), seeded, chopped coarsely
2 tablespoons tomato paste
1 teaspoon finely grated orange rind
4 sprigs fresh marjoram
1 litre (4 cups) vegetable stock, warmed
1½ cups (180g) frozen peas
150g calamari rings

1 Shell and devein prawns, leaving tails intact. Scrub mussels; remove beards. Cut fish into 3cm pieces.
2 Heat oil in large deep frying pan; cook onion and garlic, stirring, until onion softens. Add pasta and saffron; stir to coat in onion mixture. Stir in wine, tomato, paste, rind and marjoram; cook, stirring, until wine has almost evaporated.
3 Add 1 cup of the stock; stir until liquid is absorbed. Add remaining stock; cook, stirring, until pasta is almost tender.
4 Place peas and seafood in pan on top of risoni mixture; do not stir to combine. Cover pan, reduce heat; simmer about 10 minutes or until seafood has changed in colour and mussels have opened (discard any that do not).

preparation time 30 minutes
cooking time 30 minutes **serves** 4
nutritional count per serving 14.6g total fat (2.9g saturated fat); 3373kJ (807 cal); 94.6g carbohydrate; 58.1g protein; 9g fibre

This recipe can be made in a traditional paella pan if you own one, otherwise a deep frying pan or wok with a tight-fitting lid will suffice. Serve the paella straight from the pan at the table.

braised veal rolls with pasta & olives

4 large red capsicums (1.4kg)
250g spinach leaves
8 veal steaks (640g)
¼ cup (60ml) olive oil
2 medium brown onions (300g), chopped finely
2 cloves garlic, crushed
425g can tomato puree
⅓ cup (80ml) dry red wine
2 teaspoons brown sugar
½ cup (110g) risoni pasta
¾ cup (90g) seeded black olives
2 tablespoons finely sliced fresh basil

1 Quarter capsicums; discard seeds and membranes. Roast, skin-side up, under very hot grill until skin blisters and blackens. Cover capsicum pieces in plastic or paper for 5 minutes; peel away skin.
2 Place spinach leaves over each veal steak; top each steak with two capsicum pieces. Roll veal tightly; secure with toothpicks.
3 Heat 2 tablespoons of the oil in large saucepan. Cook veal, in batches, until browned all over; drain on absorbent paper. Heat remaining oil in pan; cook onion and garlic, stirring, until onion is soft.
4 Return veal to pan with puree, wine and sugar; simmer, covered, 15 minutes. Add pasta and olives; simmer, covered, about 7 minutes or until pasta is tender.
5 Serve veal sliced with sauce; sprinkle with basil. Serve with steamed green beans, if you like.

preparation time 35 minutes
cooking time 1 hour **serves** 8
nutritional count per serving 8.8g total fat (1.3g saturated fat); 1195kJ (286 cal); 23.6g carbohydrate; 23.9g protein; 4.8g fibre

mussels & beans à la grecque

1 cup (220g) risoni pasta
500g frozen broad beans
½ cup (125ml) water
½ cup (125ml) dry white wine
1kg medium mussels, scrubbed, beards removed
200g green beans, trimmed, cut into 2cm lengths
1 cup (120g) seeded black olives
1 large red capsicum (350g), chopped coarsely
oregano and red wine vinaigrette
2 teaspoons finely chopped fresh oregano
2 tablespoons red wine vinegar
2 cloves garlic, crushed
1 small brown onion (80g), grated finely
½ teaspoon ground cumin
⅓ cup (80ml) extra virgin olive oil

1 Cook pasta and broad beans, separately, in large saucepans of boiling water until tender; drain. Cool beans 10 minutes then peel away grey outer shells.
2 Meanwhile, heat the water and wine in large saucepan. Add mussels; cook, covered, about 10 minutes or until open (discard any that do not). Reserve 16 mussels; cover to keep warm. Remove remaining mussels from shells.
3 Make oregano and red wine vinaigrette.
4 Boil, steam or microwave green beans until just tender; drain. Rinse under cold water; drain.
5 Combine pasta, beans and shelled mussels in large bowl with olives, capsicum and vinaigrette; toss gently. Divide among bowls; top with mussels in shells.
oregano and red wine vinaigrette Combine ingredients in screw-top jar; shake well.

preparation time 30 minutes
cooking time 15 minutes **serves** 4
nutritional count per serving 20.6g total fat
(3.1g saturated fat); 2140kJ (512 cal); 53.3g carbohydrate;
19.3g protein; 7.5g fibre

pea & ham soup with risoni

2 teaspoons olive oil
1 medium brown onion (150g), chopped coarsely
2 teaspoons ground cumin
2.5 litres (10 cups) water
2 stalks celery (300g), trimmed, chopped coarsely
2 dried bay leaves
1.5kg ham bone
1 cup (220g) risoni pasta
2 cups (240g) frozen peas
2 tablespoons finely chopped fresh mint

1 Heat oil in large saucepan; cook onion, stirring, until softened. Add cumin; cook, stirring, until fragrant. Add the water, celery, bay leaves and ham bone; bring to the boil. Simmer, covered, 1 hour, skimming occasionally.
2 Remove bone; when cool enough to handle, cut ham from bone; discard skin, fat and bone. Shred ham finely.
3 Return soup to the boil; stir in ham, pasta and peas. Cook, uncovered, about 5 minutes or until pasta is tender. Sprinkle bowls of soup with mint.

preparation time 15 minutes
cooking time 1 hour 15 minutes **serves** 6
nutritional count per serving 3g total fat
(0.6g saturated fat); 811kJ (194 cal);
30g carbohydrate; 9g protein; 4.6g fibre

risoni with spinach & semi-dried tomatoes

30g butter
2 medium brown onions (300g), chopped finely
3 cloves garlic, crushed
500g risoni pasta
4 cups (1 litre) chicken stock (*see note, below*)
½ cup (125ml) dry white wine
150g semi-dried tomatoes, halved
100g baby spinach leaves
⅓ cup (25g) finely grated parmesan cheese

1 Melt butter in large saucepan; cook onion and garlic, stirring, until onion softens. Add pasta; stir to coat in butter mixture. Stir in stock and wine; bring to the boil.
2 Reduce heat; simmer over medium heat, stirring, until liquid is absorbed and pasta is just tender. Gently stir in tomato, spinach and cheese.

preparation time 10 minutes
cooking time 20 minutes **serves** 4
nutritional count per serving 12.4g total fat (6.3g saturated fat); 2830kJ (677 cal); 104.7g carbohydrate; 24.8g protein; 11.2g fibre

To make this a meal suitable for vegetarians, substitute vegetable stock for the chicken stock.

spaghetti

The king of pastas, spaghetti appears on menus worldwide.
Versatile and easy to cook, it seems every region of Italy has
created its own sauce to accompany this favourite.

spaghetti bolognese

1 tablespoon olive oil
2 large brown onions (400g), chopped finely
4 cloves garlic, crushed
1.2kg beef mince
2 large carrots (360g), grated coarsely
⅓ cup (95g) tomato paste
3 cups (750ml) beef stock
2 x 810g cans crushed tomatoes
1 tablespoon mixed dried herbs
500g spaghetti
¼ cup (20g) grated parmesan cheese

1 Heat oil in large saucepan; cook onion and garlic,
stirring, until onion softens.
2 Add mince; cook, stirring, until browned. Add carrot
and tomato paste; cook, stirring, 5 minutes. Add stock,
undrained tomato and herbs; bring to the boil. Reduce
heat; simmer, covered, 45 minutes, stirring occasionally.
Uncover; simmer a further 45 minutes or until mixture is
thickened slightly.
3 About 10 minutes before sauce is ready, cook pasta
in large saucepan of boiling water until tender; drain.
4 Serve half the bolognese with spaghetti, reserve
remaining half for later use (*see note, below*). Serve
sprinkled with cheese.

preparation time 15 minutes
cooking time 1 hour 40 minutes **serves** 4
nutritional count per serving 9.9g total fat
(3.9g saturated fat); 1642kJ (393 cal); 49.1g carbohydrate;
23.9g protein; 4.6g fibre

This recipe makes a double quantity of the bolognese
sauce. Freeze any leftover bolognese sauce for up
to three months. The leftover sauce can be used for
the *beef, garlic and silver beet pasta bake* on page 52.

prosciutto-wrapped chicken with spaghetti

8 chicken thigh fillets (800g)
¼ cup (20g) grated parmesan cheese
1 tablespoon coarsely chopped fresh oregano
200g mozzarella cheese, coarsely chopped
8 slices prosciutto (120g)
2 tablespoons olive oil
1 clove garlic, crushed
6 medium tomatoes (900g), chopped coarsely
1 small brown onion (80g), chopped finely
¼ cup (60ml) chicken stock
2 teaspoons balsamic vinegar
375g spaghetti
1 tablespoon coarsely chopped fresh flat-leaf parsley

1 Lightly pound fillets using meat mallet. Sprinkle fillets with combined parmesan and oregano; top with mozzarella. Roll tightly; secure with toothpicks. Wrap prosciutto firmly around open ends to secure cheese.
2 Heat half the oil in large saucepan; cook chicken, in batches, until browned all over.
3 Heat remaining oil in pan; cook garlic, tomato and onion, stirring, about 5 minutes or until onion is soft.
4 Return chicken to pan. Add stock and vinegar; simmer, covered, 10 minutes. Turn chicken; simmer, uncovered, about 10 minutes or until chicken is tender. Stir in parsley; remove and discard toothpicks.
5 Meanwhile, cook pasta in large saucepan of boiling water until tender; drain.
6 Place pasta in serving bowl; top with chicken.

preparation time 35 minutes
cooking time 40 minutes **serves** 4
nutritional count per serving 39.2g total fat (14.6g saturated fat); 3879kJ (928 cal); 69.7g carbohydrate; 70.8g protein; 6.2g fibre

spaghetti with mussels & clams

500g mussels
500g clams
¼ cup (60ml) dry white wine
¼ cup (60ml) water
500g spaghetti
⅓ cup (80ml) extra virgin olive oil
2 cloves garlic, crushed
1 fresh small red thai chilli, chopped finely
2 medium tomatoes (300g), seeded,
    chopped coarsely
½ cup coarsely chopped fresh flat-leaf parsley

1 Scrub mussels; remove beards. Rinse clams.
2 Combine wine and the water in large saucepan;
bring to the boil. Add mussels and clams; reduce heat.
Simmer, covered, until shells open (discard any that do
not). Remove seafood from liquid; cover to keep warm.
Strain cooking liquid through fine sieve into medium
heatproof jug; reserve ⅓ cup (80ml) of the liquid.
3 Cook pasta in large saucepan of boiling water until
tender; drain. Return to pan.
4 Meanwhile, heat oil in large frying pan; cook garlic
and chilli, stirring, until fragrant. Add tomatoes and
reserved cooking liquid; simmer, uncovered, until hot.
5 Add seafood, tomato mixture and parsley to pasta;
toss gently.

preparation time 20 minutes
cooking time 15 minutes **serves** 6
nutritional count per serving 13.5g total fat
(2g saturated fat); 1818kJ (435 cal); 59.2g carbohydrate;
15g protein; 3.9g fibre

spaghetti & meatballs

2 tablespoons olive oil
2 cloves garlic, crushed
1 medium brown onion (150g), sliced thinly
½ cup (125ml) dry red wine
2 cups (520g) bottled tomato pasta sauce
½ cup (125ml) chicken stock
¼ cup coarsely chopped fresh basil
375g spaghetti
⅓ cup (25g) flaked parmesan cheese
meatballs
1kg beef mince
1 small green capsicum (150g), chopped finely
1 small brown onion (80g), chopped finely
2 cloves garlic, crushed
¼ cup coarsely chopped fresh flat-leaf parsley
1 egg
1 cup (70g) stale breadcrumbs
1 teaspoon finely grated lemon rind
½ cup (130g) sun-dried tomato pesto

1 Make meatballs.
2 Heat oil in large frying pan; cook meatballs, in batches, until browned all over. Drain on absorbent paper.
3 Cook garlic and onion in same pan, stirring, until onion softens. Add wine; bring to the boil. Reduce heat; simmer, uncovered, about 5 minutes or until mixture is reduced by half. Add sauce and stock; bring to the boil.
4 Return meatballs to pan, reduce heat; simmer, uncovered, about 10 minutes or until meatballs are cooked through. Stir in basil.
5 Meanwhile, cook pasta in large saucepan of boiling water until tender; drain.
6 Divide pasta among serving bowls; top with meatballs and sauce, serve with cheese.
meatballs Combine ingredients in large bowl; roll level tablespoons of mince mixture into balls (*see note, below*).

preparation time 20 minutes
cooking time 20 minutes **serves** 4
nutritional count per serving 50.7g total fat (16.1g saturated fat); 5133kJ (1228 cal); 113g carbohydrate; 70g protein; 9g fibre

We've made twice the number of meatballs required to serve four; freeze half the meatballs for future use by placing the uncooked meatballs in a single layer on a tray, cover; freeze until solid. Remove meatballs from tray and place in either a storage container that has a tight-fitting lid, or a sealable plastic bag; return to freezer. Frozen meatballs can be thawed, then cooked directly in the pasta sauce.

spaghetti marinara

1 tablespoon olive oil
1 medium brown onion (150g), chopped finely
⅓ cup (80ml) dry white wine
⅓ cup (95g) tomato paste
850g can crushed tomatoes
750g seafood marinara mix
¼ cup coarsely chopped fresh flat-leaf parsley
375g spaghetti

1 Heat oil in large frying pan; cook onion until soft.
2 Add wine, paste and undrained tomatoes to pan; bring to the boil. Reduce heat; simmer, uncovered, 10 minutes or until sauce thickens slightly.
3 Add marinara mix to tomato mixture; cook, stirring occasionally, about 5 minutes or until seafood is cooked through. Stir in parsley.
4 Meanwhile, cook pasta in large saucepan of boiling water until tender; drain. Serve marinara over pasta.

preparation time 5 minutes
cooking time 15 minutes **serves** 4
nutritional count per serving 11.6g total fat
(2.3g saturated fat); 2847kJ (681 cal); 76.4g carbohydrate; 59.7g protein; 7.3g fibre

spaghetti napoletana

2 teaspoons olive oil
1 small brown onion (80g), chopped finely
3 cloves garlic, crushed
850g can crushed tomatoes
¼ cup coarsely chopped, firmly packed fresh basil
⅓ cup coarsely chopped fresh flat-leaf parsley
375g spaghetti

1 Heat oil in large saucepan; cook onion and garlic, stirring, until onion softens.
2 Add undrained tomatoes; bring to the boil. Reduce heat; simmer, uncovered, about 20 minutes or until reduced by about a third. Stir in basil and parsley.
3 Meanwhile, cook pasta in large saucepan of boiling water until tender; drain. Serve pasta topped with sauce.

preparation time 5 minutes
cooking time 25 minutes **serves** 4
nutritional count per serving 3.8g total fat
(0.5g saturated fat); 1630kJ (390 cal); 71.9g carbohydrate; 12.8g protein; 6.6g fibre

If you cook this sauce even longer, until it reduces by half, it makes a good pizza-base sauce or, with capers stirred through it, a delicious topping for chicken or veal scaloppine.

spaghetti puttanesca

¼ cup (60ml) olive oil
2 cloves garlic, crushed
4 medium tomatoes (600g), chopped coarsely
½ cup finely chopped fresh flat-leaf parsley
12 stuffed olives, sliced thinly
45g can anchovy fillets, drained, chopped finely
1 tablespoon finely chopped fresh basil
pinch chilli powder
375g spaghetti

1 Heat oil in medium saucepan; cook garlic until just changed in colour.
2 Add tomato, parsley, olives, anchovy, basil and chilli powder; cook, stirring, 3 minutes.
3 Meanwhile, cook pasta in large saucepan of boiling water until tender; drain.
4 Combine pasta in large bowl with sauce; toss gently.

preparation time 15 minutes
cooking time 20 minutes **serves** 4
nutritional count per serving 16.5g total fat
(2.4g saturated fat); 2065kJ (494 cal); 67.2g carbohydrate;
15.4g protein; 6.5g fibre

spaghetti with pesto

2 cups coarsely chopped fresh basil
2 tablespoons roasted pine nuts
2 cloves garlic
⅓ cup (80ml) olive oil
¼ cup (20g) grated parmesan cheese
375g spaghetti

1 Blend or process basil, nuts and garlic until smooth. With processor operating, add oil in a thin steady stream; process until mixture is combined. Place pesto in medium bowl; stir in cheese.
2 Cook pasta in large saucepan of boiling water until tender; drain.
3 Combine pasta with pesto in large bowl; toss gently. Serve with flakes of parmesan cheese, if you like.

preparation time 15 minutes
cooking time 15 minutes **serves** 4
nutritional count per serving 26g total fat
(4.1g saturated fat); 2328kJ (557 cal); 65g carbohydrate;
13.7g protein; 4.3g fibre

pasta salads

Once just a useful way of using up leftover pasta, these days versatile pasta salads can star on their own as a main dish, or add pizzazz as a side dish.

gremolata lamb salad

250g farfalle pasta
600g asparagus, trimmed, halved crossways
200g green beans, trimmed, halved crossways
1 tablespoon vegetable oil
800g lamb fillets
2 teaspoons dijon mustard
3 shallots (75g), sliced thinly
⅓ cup (50g) roasted pine nuts
⅓ cup loosely packed fresh flat-leaf parsley leaves
lemon dijon dressing
2 tablespoons lemon juice
2 tablespoons extra virgin olive oil
2 teaspoons dijon mustard
gremolata
2 cloves garlic, chopped finely
1 tablespoon finely grated lemon rind
½ cup finely chopped fresh flat-leaf parsley

1 Make lemon dijon dressing and gremolata.
2 Cook pasta in large saucepan of boiling water until tender; drain. Rinse under cold water; drain.
3 Meanwhile, boil, steam or microwave asparagus and beans, separately, until just tender; drain.
4 Heat oil in large frying pan; cook lamb, uncovered, until browned and cooked as desired. Spread mustard over lamb; press gremolata firmly onto mustard. Cover; stand 5 minutes. Slice lamb thickly.
5 Place pasta, asparagus, beans and lamb in large bowl with shallots, nuts, parsley and dressing; toss gently.
lemon dijon dressing Combine ingredients in screw-top jar; shake well.
gremolata Combine ingredients in small bowl.

preparation time 20 minutes
cooking time 20 minutes **serves** 4
nutritional count per serving 41.2g total fat (10.5g saturated fat); 3315kJ (793 cal); 47.4g carbohydrate; 55g protein; 7.1g fibre

Farfalle is a bow-tie shaped short pasta sometimes known as butterfly or bow-tie pasta.

pasta salad with green beans & tuna

375g large pasta spirals
250g green beans, trimmed, halved crossways
425g canned tuna in oil
1 medium red capsicum (200g), sliced thinly
¾ cup loosely packed fresh flat-leaf parsley leaves
lemon dressing
2 cloves garlic, crushed
1 tablespoon finely grated lemon rind
1 teaspoon cracked black pepper
1 tablespoon lemon juice

1 Cook pasta in large saucepan of boiling water until tender; drain. Rinse under cold water; drain.
2 Meanwhile, boil, steam or microwave beans until just tender; drain. Rinse under cold water; drain.
3 Drain tuna over small bowl; reserve oil for dressing. Flake tuna into large chunks with fork.
4 Make lemon dressing.
5 Place pasta, beans and tuna in large bowl with dressing and remaining ingredients; toss gently.
lemon dressing Combine ingredients with reserved oil in screw-top jar; shake well.

preparation time 10 minutes
cooking time 10 minutes **serves** 4
nutritional count per serving 26g total fat
(3.9g saturated fat); 2750kJ (658 cal); 67.5g carbohydrate;
35g protein; 6.2g fibre

curried macaroni tuna & bean salad

250g small macaroni pasta
200g green beans, halved
200g yellow string beans, halved
415g can tuna in oil, drained, flaked
1 small red onion (80g), sliced thinly
¼ cup finely chopped fresh flat-leaf parsley
½ cup (125ml) olive oil
¼ cup (60ml) lemon juice
2 cloves garlic, crushed
2 teaspoons curry powder

1 Cook pasta in large saucepan of boiling water until tender; drain. Rinse under cold water; drain.
2 Meanwhile, boil, steam or microwave beans until just tender; drain. Rinse under cold water; drain.
3 Place pasta and beans in large bowl with tuna, onion, parsley and combined remaining ingredients; toss gently.

preparation time 15 minutes
cooking time 15 minutes **serves** 4
nutritional count per serving 41.1g total fat
(6g saturated fat); 2876kJ (688 cal); 46.9g carbohydrate;
30.4g protein; 5.7g fibre

curried pasta salad

1 cup (180g) small pasta shells
1 medium red capsicum (200g), chopped finely
1 medium green capsicum (200g), chopped finely
2 tablespoons finely chopped fresh chives
100g button mushrooms, chopped finely
curry dressing
2 teaspoons curry powder
1 tablespoon caster sugar
½ cup (125ml) peanut oil
¼ cup (60ml) white vinegar
1 tablespoon cream

1 Cook pasta in large saucepan of boiling water until tender; drain.
2 Meanwhile, make curry dressing.
3 Place pasta in large bowl with capsicum, chives and mushrooms. Add dressing; toss to combine.
curry dressing Place curry powder and sugar in small bowl; gradually whisk in oil, vinegar and cream.

preparation time 10 minutes
cooking time 10 minutes **serves** 4
nutritional count per serving 31.3g total fat (6.7g saturated fat); 1969kJ (471 cal); 39.2g carbohydrate; 7.4g protein; 3g fibre

russian penne salad

375g penne pasta
2 cups (240g) frozen peas
450g can whole baby beetroot, drained, chopped coarsely
6 green onions, chopped finely
2 cloves garlic, crushed
2 large dill pickles, chopped finely
¼ cup coarsely chopped fresh flat-leaf parsley
1 cup (240g) sour cream
1 cup (250ml) buttermilk

1 Cook pasta in large saucepan of boiling water until tender; drain. Rinse under cold water; drain.
2 Meanwhile, boil, steam or microwave peas until just tender; drain.
3 Place pasta and peas in large bowl with beetroot, onion, garlic, pickle, parsley and combined cream and buttermilk; toss gently.

preparation time 15 minutes
cooking time 10 minutes **serves** 4
nutritional count per serving 26.6g total fat (16.7g saturated fat); 2759kJ (660 cal); 80.6g carbohydrate; 19.6g protein; 9.6g fibre

greek penne salad

250g penne pasta
250g fetta cheese
4 medium tomatoes (600g), seeded, sliced thinly
½ lebanese cucumber (130g), seeded, sliced thinly
1 small red onion (100g), sliced thinly
¾ cup (120g) kalamata olives, seeded
¾ cup (120g) large green olives, seeded
⅓ cup (80ml) olive oil
⅓ cup (80ml) white vinegar
1 teaspoon white sugar
2 tablespoons finely chopped fresh flat-leaf parsley

1 Cook pasta in large saucepan of boiling water until tender; drain. Rinse under cold water; drain.
2 Meanwhile, cut the cheese into baton-shapes pieces about the same size as the pasta.
3 Place pasta and cheese in large bowl with tomato, cucumber, onion, olives and combined remaining ingredients; toss gently.

preparation time 15 minutes
cooking time 15 minutes **serves** 4
nutritional count per serving 34.3g total fat (12.4g saturated fat); 2717kJ (650 cal); 62.2g carbohydrate; 20.6g protein; 5.4g fibre

Goes well with lemon-marinated lamb skewers.

mediterranean pasta salad

375g elbow macaroni pasta
350g artichoke hearts in oil
400g semi-dried tomatoes
¼ cup loosely packed fresh oregano
400g mozzarella cheese, chopped coarsely
¼ cup (60ml) sherry vinegar
2 cloves garlic, crushed

1 Cook pasta in large saucepan of boiling water until tender; drain. Rinse under cold water; drain.
2 Meanwhile, drain artichokes over small bowl; reserve 2 tablespoons of the oil, discard remaining oil.
3 Quarter artichokes; place in large bowl with pasta, tomatoes, oregano, cheese and combined vinegar, garlic and reserved oil; toss gently.

preparation time 10 minutes
cooking time 15 minutes **serves** 4
nutritional count per serving 31.1g total fat (15.2g saturated fat); 3808kJ (911 cal); 99g carbohydrate; 48.6g protein; 19.4g fibre

This salad is great picnic food.

pasta salad with chicken livers & pistachios

250g curly lasagne
500g chicken livers, trimmed
150g baby rocket leaves
1 tablespoon finely grated lemon rind
⅓ cup (45g) roasted pistachios
lemon mustard dressing
2 teaspoons dijon mustard
1 clove garlic, crushed
⅓ cup (80ml) olive oil
¼ cup (60ml) lemon juice

1 Cook pasta in large saucepan of boiling water until tender; drain. Rinse under cold water; drain. Cut pasta lengthways into 2cm-thick ribbons.
2 Meanwhile, make lemon mustard dressing.
3 Halve chicken livers; cook, in batches, in heated oiled large frying pan about 2 minutes or until browned and cooked as desired (*see note, below*).
4 Place pasta and liver in large bowl with dressing and remaining ingredients; toss gently.
lemon mustard dressing Combine ingredients in screw-top jar; shake well.

preparation time 10 minutes
cooking time 15 minutes **serves** 4
nutritional count per serving 29.8g total fat (5g saturated fat); 2512kJ (601 cal); 48.5g carbohydrate; 32.9g protein; 3.9g fibre

Be sure not to overcook the chicken livers or they will be dry and unappealing.

roasted capsicum, goats cheese & walnut salad

375g large spiral pasta
2 medium red capsicums (400g)
2 medium yellow capsicums (400g)
150g goats cheese, crumbled
⅓ cup (35g) walnuts, roasted, chopped coarsely
½ cup loosely packed fresh basil leaves
¼ cup (60ml) red wine vinegar
⅓ cup (80ml) olive oil
1 clove garlic, crushed
2 teaspoons wholegrain mustard

1 Cook pasta in large saucepan of boiling water until tender; drain. Rinse under cold water; drain.
2 Meanwhile, quarter capsicums; discard seeds and membranes. Roast, skin-side up, under very hot grill until skin blisters and blackens. Cover capsicum pieces in plastic or paper for 5 minutes; peel away skin then slice thickly.
3 Place pasta and capsicum in large bowl with cheese, nuts, basil and combined vinegar, oil, garlic and mustard; toss gently.

preparation time 10 minutes
cooking time 20 minutes **serves** 4
nutritional count per serving 31.5g total fat (7g saturated fat); 2738kJ (655 cal); 70.4g carbohydrate; 23.8g protein; 5.7g fibre

Fetta or any soft, crumbly cheese can be substituted for the goats cheese, and roasted pecan halves can be used instead of the walnuts.

salmon pasta salad with lemon mayonnaise

250g orecchiette pasta
20 caperberries (100g), rinsed, drained
2 x 400g cans red salmon, drained, flaked
1 large white onion (200g), halved, sliced thinly
4 stalks celery (600g), trimmed, sliced thinly
4 large red cabbage leaves, trimmed
lemon mayonnaise
2 tablespoons water
⅔ cup (200g) mayonnaise
½ cup (120g) sour cream
¼ cup (60ml) lemon juice
¼ cup coarsely chopped fresh dill

1 Cook pasta in large saucepan of boiling water until tender; drain. Rinse under cold water; drain.
2 Meanwhile, make lemon mayonnaise.
3 Slice eight caperberries thinly; combine in large bowl with salmon, onion, celery, pasta and half the mayonnaise; toss gently.
4 Divide cabbage among serving bowls; fill with salad, top with remaining mayonnaise and caperberries.
lemon mayonnaise Whisk ingredients in small bowl until well combined.

preparation time 15 minutes
cooking time 10 minutes **serves** 4
nutritional count per serving 48.5g total fat (15.1g saturated fat); 3641kJ (871 cal); 60.6g carbohydrate; 45.7g protein; 6.1g fibre

farfalle with baked salmon, caperberries & dill

2 large red onions (600g), cut into wedges
1 cup (160g) caperberries, rinsed, drained
cooking-oil spray
1 fresh small red thai chilli, chopped finely
¼ cup finely chopped fresh dill
2 teaspoons olive oil
1kg piece skinless salmon fillet
500g farfalle pasta
⅔ cup (160ml) dry white wine
2 tablespoons lemon juice
½ cup (125ml) cream
250g baby rocket leaves

1 Preheat oven to 200°C/180°C fan-forced.
2 Place onion, in single layer, in large baking dish with caperberries. Spray lightly with oil; roast, uncovered, about 25 minutes or until onion is softened.
3 Combine chilli, half the dill and oil in small bowl. Place salmon on large baking-paper lined oven tray; brush salmon both sides with chilli mixture. Roast, uncovered, about 10 minutes or until salmon is just tender and cooked as desired.
4 Cook pasta in large pan of boiling water until tender.
5 Combine wine and juice in small pan; bring to the boil. Simmer, uncovered, about 5 minutes or until liquid reduces by half. Stir in cream and remaining dill.
6 Place drained pasta, flaked salmon, onion mixture and dill cream sauce in large bowl with rocket; toss gently.

preparation time 25 minutes
cooking time 30 minutes **serves** 8
nutritional count per serving 18.3g total fat
(6.8g saturated fat); 2174kJ (520 cal); 49.6g carbohydrate;
33.7g protein; 3.8g fibre

ravioli salad

375g packaged spinach and ricotta ravioli
4 rindless bacon rashers (260g), chopped coarsely
3 cups (250g) broccoli florets
250g cherry tomatoes, halved
2 tablespoons finely sliced fresh basil
½ cup (125ml) olive oil
¼ cup (60ml) white wine vinegar
2 tablespoons sun-dried tomato pesto

1 Cook pasta in large saucepan of boiling water until pasta floats to the top. Rinse under cold water; drain.
2 Meanwhile, cook bacon in small frying pan, stirring, until browned and crisp; drain on absorbent paper.
3 Boil, steam or microwave broccoli until just tender, drain. Rinse under cold water; drain.
4 Place pasta, bacon and broccoli in large bowl with tomato, basil and combined remaining ingredients; toss gently.

preparation time 15 minutes
cooking time 15 minutes **serves** 4
nutritional count per serving 45.9g total fat
(9.9g saturated fat); 2399kJ (573 cal); 15.1g carbohydrate; 23.8g protein; 5.2g fibre

Use any variety of ravioli you like so long as the filling does not include any meat.
You can use any kind of prepared pesto in this salad's dressing – roasted vegetable pesto is a good alternative.
You need approximately 500g of untrimmed fresh broccoli to get the amount of florets needed for this recipe.

pasta with the lot

250g curly lasagne
150g salami, sliced thickly
200g swiss brown mushrooms, sliced thickly
1 medium green capsicum (200g), sliced thinly
2 medium tomatoes (300g), seeded, sliced thinly
4 drained anchovies, chopped coarsely
100g kalamata olives, seeded
½ cup (125ml) vegetable or tomato juice
¼ cup (60ml) red wine vinegar
¼ cup (60ml) olive oil
2 cloves garlic, crushed

1 Cook pasta in large saucepan of boiling water until tender; drain. Rinse under cold water; drain.
2 Place pasta in large bowl with salami, mushrooms, capsicum, tomato, anchovy, olives and combined remaining ingredients; toss gently.

preparation time 10 minutes
cooking time 15 minutes **serves** 4
nutritional count per serving 29.2g total fat (6.8g saturated fat); 2374kJ (568 cal); 53.8g carbohydrate; 19.9g protein; 5.3g fibre

We used a hot and spicy spanish salami in this recipe but you could use milder cabanossi or pepperoni, if you prefer.

smoked salmon & dill salad

250g linguine pasta
2 small fennel bulbs (400g), trimmed, sliced thinly
1 medium red onion (170g), sliced thinly
200g smoked salmon, sliced thickly
¼ cup rinsed, drained capers, chopped coarsely
½ cup loosely packed fresh dill
½ cup (120ml) crème fraîche
2 teaspoons finely grated lemon rind
¼ cup (60ml) lemon juice

1 Cook pasta in large saucepan of boiling water until tender; drain. Rinse under cold water; drain.
2 Place pasta in large bowl with fennel, onion, salmon, capers, dill and combined remaining ingredients; toss gently to combine.

preparation time 10 minutes
cooking time 15 minutes **serves** 4
nutritional count per serving 15.2g total fat (8.5g saturated fat); 1777kJ (425 cal); 49g carbohydrate; 20.5g protein; 4.4g fibre

The salad can be prepared several hours ahead; keep, covered, in the refrigerator. Pour over combined crème fraîche, rind and juice just before serving. You can replace the crème fraîche with sour cream, light sour cream or double cream if you prefer.

sweet chilli prawn pasta salad

250g rigatoni pasta
1kg cooked large prawns, shelled, tails intact
2 green onions, chopped finely
1 tablespoon coarsely chopped watercress
1 tablespoon coarsely chopped fresh coriander
½ lebanese cucumber (130g), chopped coarsely
½ cup (125ml) sweet chilli sauce
1 teaspoon sesame oil
1 tablespoon lime juice

1 Cook pasta in large saucepan of boiling water until tender; drain. Rinse under cold water; drain.
2 Place pasta in large bowl with prawns, onion, watercress, coriander, cucumber and combined remaining ingredients; toss gently to combine.

preparation time 10 minutes
cooking time 10 minutes **serves** 4
nutritional count per serving 3.5g total fat (0.6g saturated fat); 1572kJ (376 cal); 59.8g carbohydrate; 33.3g protein; 4.1g fibre

spinach & prosciutto pasta salad

375g large pasta spirals
12 slices prosciutto (180g)
150g baby spinach leaves
2 tablespoons wholegrain mustard
2 cloves garlic, crushed
½ cup (125ml) olive oil
¼ cup (60ml) lemon juice

1 Cook pasta in large saucepan of boiling water until tender; drain. Rinse under cold water; drain.
2 Meanwhile, cook prosciutto, in batches, in heated oiled large frying pan until browned and crisp; drain on absorbent paper, chop coarsely.
3 Place pasta and prosciutto in large bowl with spinach and combined remaining ingredients; toss gently.

preparation time 10 minutes
cooking time 10 minutes **serves** 4
nutritional count per serving 32.4g total fat
(5.2g saturated fat); 2684kJ (642 cal); 65.3g carbohydrate;
20.1g protein; 4.6g fibre

Finely slice or chop two hard-boiled eggs, if you wish, and toss them through this salad just before serving.

chicken, hazelnut & rocket salad

250g linguine pasta
340g chicken breast fillets
½ cup (70g) hazelnuts, roasted, chopped coarsely
100g curly endive
150g baby rocket leaves
⅓ cup (80ml) lime juice
⅓ cup (80ml) olive oil
2 cloves garlic, crushed
2 teaspoons dijon mustard

1 Cook pasta in large saucepan of boiling water until tender; drain. Rinse pasta under cold water; drain.
2 Meanwhile, cook chicken on heated oiled grill plate (or grill or barbecue) until browned all over and cooked through. Stand 5 minutes; cut into thin slices.
3 Combine pasta and chicken in large bowl with nuts, endive, rocket and combined remaining ingredients; toss gently.

preparation time 5 minutes
cooking time 15 minutes **serves** 4
nutritional count per serving 34.8g total fat
(4.6g saturated fat); 2596kJ (621 cal); 45g carbohydrate;
29.6g protein; 5.4g fibre

pasta caesar salad

200g large pasta shells
2 rindless bacon rashers (130g), chopped finely
1 medium cos lettuce, torn
2 hard-boiled eggs, chopped coarsely
2 small avocados (400g), chopped coarsely
½ cup (40g) shaved parmesan cheese
caesar dressing
1 egg
2 cloves garlic, quartered
2 tablespoons lemon juice
1 teaspoon dijon mustard
8 drained anchovy fillets
¾ cup (180ml) olive oil

1 Cook pasta in large saucepan of boiling water until tender; drain. Rinse under cold water; drain.
2 Meanwhile, make caesar dressing.
3 Cook bacon in small frying pan, stirring, until browned and crisp; drain on absorbent paper.
4 Place pasta and bacon in large bowl with lettuce, egg and avocado; pour over half the caesar dressing, toss gently.
5 Divide salad among serving plates; drizzle with remaining dressing, sprinkle with cheese.
caesar dressing Blend or process egg, garlic, juice, mustard and anchovies until smooth. With motor operating, gradually add oil in a thin steady stream; process until dressing thickens.

preparation time 15 minutes
cooking time 15 minutes **serves** 4
nutritional count per serving 70.1g total fat (14.3g saturated fat); 3766kJ (901 cal); 38.7g carbohydrate; 27.1g protein; 7.2g fibre

seafood pasta salad

1 teaspoon olive oil
1 small brown onion (80g), sliced thinly
1 clove garlic, crushed
500g seafood marinara mix
375g large pasta shells
1 tablespoon dry white wine
½ cup (150g) mayonnaise
1 teaspoon lemon juice
2 teaspoons worcestershire sauce
⅓ cup (80ml) tomato sauce
¼ teaspoon Tabasco sauce
1 tablespoon coarsely chopped fresh flat-leaf parsley
100g baby rocket leaves

1 Heat oil in large frying pan; cook onion and garlic, stirring, until onion softens. Add marinara mix; cook, stirring, about 5 minutes or until seafood is cooked through. Place marinara mixture in large bowl, cover; refrigerate until cold.
2 Cook pasta in large saucepan of boiling water until tender; drain. Rinse under cold water; drain.
3 Place pasta and combined wine, mayonnaise, juice, sauces and parsley in bowl with marinara mixture; toss gently to combine. Serve seafood salad on rocket leaves.

preparation time 5 minutes (plus refrigeration time)
cooking time 20 minutes **serves** 4
nutritional count per serving 18.2g total fat
(2.7g saturated fat); 2809kJ (672 cal); 80.1g carbohydrate;
42.9g protein; 4.5g fibre

lamb & pasta with walnut coriander pesto

375g farfalle pasta

4 lamb fillets (400g)

1½ cups firmly packed, coarsely chopped fresh coriander (*see note, below*)

½ cup (50g) walnuts, roasted

½ cup (40g) coarsely grated parmesan cheese

2 cloves garlic, quartered

½ cup (125ml) light olive oil

1 tablespoon drained preserved lemon, chopped finely

½ cup (140g) yogurt

2 teaspoons light olive oil, extra

2 teaspoons lemon juice

1 Cook pasta in large saucepan of boiling water until tender; drain. Rinse under cold water; drain.

2 Meanwhile, cook lamb in heated oiled large frying pan until cooked as desired.

3 Reserve 2 tablespoons of coriander leaves. Blend or process remaining coriander, nuts, cheese, garlic and oil until mixture forms a smooth paste. Combine pesto with pasta in large bowl.

4 Divide pasta among serving plates, top with thinly sliced lamb and preserved lemon; drizzle with combined yogurt, extra oil and juice, then top with reserved coriander leaves.

preparation time 10 minutes
cooking time 15 minutes **serves** 4
nutritional count per serving 48.5g total fat (9.5g saturated fat); 3624kJ (867 cal); 66.8g carbohydrate; 38.9g protein; 4.9g fibre

You need two bunches of fresh coriander, including the roots and stems as well as the leaves.

farfalle with asparagus & grilled haloumi

250g farfalle pasta
750g asparagus, trimmed, chopped coarsely
250g haloumi cheese, sliced thinly
1 medium avocado (250g), sliced thinly
2 tablespoons coarsely chopped fresh chives
1 tablespoon finely grated lemon rind
¼ cup (60ml) lemon juice
⅓ cup (80ml) olive oil
1 teaspoon white sugar

1 Cook pasta in large saucepan of boiling water until tender; drain. Rinse under cold water; drain.
2 Meanwhile, boil, steam or microwave asparagus until just tender; drain well.
3 Cook haloumi, in batches, in medium frying pan until browned lightly; drain on absorbent paper.
4 Place pasta, asparagus and haloumi in large bowl with avocado, chives and combined remaining ingredients; toss gently.

preparation time 10 minutes
cooking time 20 minutes **serves** 4
nutritional count per serving 39.6g total fat (11.7g saturated fat); 2721kJ (651 cal); 47.3g carbohydrate; 24.5g protein; 4.8g fibre

Instead of boiling the asparagus, break off the woody ends then halve the spears and cook them on a lightly oiled grill plate or under a grill until just tender and browned lightly.

glossary

ARTICHOKE HEARTS tender centre of the globe artichoke. Purchase fresh, or in oil or brine in glass jars.

BASIL an aromatic herb; there are many types, but the most commonly used is sweet, or common, basil.

BEANS
broad also known as fava or windsor beans; available dried, fresh, canned or frozen. Fresh or frozen, they are best peeled twice, discarding both the outer long green pod and the beige-green tough inner shell.
kidney medium-size red bean, slightly floury in texture yet sweet in flavour; sold dried or canned.
sprouts tender new growths of assorted beans and seeds germinated for consumption. The most readily available are mung beans, soya beans, alfalfa and snow pea sprouts.
BUK CHOY also known as bok choy, pak choi, chinese white cabbage and chinese chard, has a mild mustard taste. Baby buk choy is smaller and more tender.

BUTTERMILK originally the term given to the slightly sour liquid left after butter was churned from cream, today it is commercially made similarly to yogurt. Sold alongside all fresh milk products in supermarkets; despite the implication of its name, it is low in fat.

CAPERBERRIES fruit formed after the caper buds have flowered; they are pickled, usually with stalks intact.

CAPERS the grey-green buds of a warm climate shrub, sold either dried and salted or pickled in a vinegar brine.

CHEESE
brie smooth and rich, brie has a bloomy white rind and a creamy centre that becomes runnier as it ripens.
cheddar the most widely eaten cheese in the world, cheddar is a semi-hard cows-milk cheese. It ranges in colour from white to pale yellow and has a slightly crumbly texture when matured.
fetta a white cheese with milky, fresh acidity. Most commonly made from cows milk, though sheep and goats milk varieties are available. Fetta is matured in brine for at least a month, which imparts a strong salty flavour. Fetta is solid but crumbles readily.
goats cheese made from goats milk, has an earthy, strong taste; available in both soft and firm textures; is sometimes rolled in ash or herbs.

gorgonzola originally from the Lombardy region of Italy; a creamy, cows-milk blue-moulded cheese.
haloumi a firm, cream-coloured sheep-milk cheese matured in brine; like a salty fetta in flavour. Should be eaten while still warm as it becomes tough on cooling.
mascarpone a cultured cream product. Whitish to creamy yellow in colour, it has a soft, creamy texture, a high fat content and a tangy taste.
mozzarella a semi-soft cheese with a delicate, fresh taste; has a low melting point and stringy texture when hot.
parmesan also known as parmigiano, is a hard, grainy cheese. The curd is salted in brine for a month before being aged for up to two years in humid conditions.
pecorino the generic Italian name for cheeses made from sheep milk. It's a hard, white to pale yellow cheese. Use parmesan, if unavailable.
pizza cheese a blend of grated mozzarella, cheddar and parmesan.
ricotta a sweet, fairly moist, fresh curd cheese having a low fat content.

CHILLIES available in many types and sizes. Wear rubber gloves to seed and chop fresh chillies as they can burn your skin. Removing membranes and seeds lessens the heat level.
cayenne pepper a thin-fleshed, long, extremely hot red chilli; usually purchased dried and ground.
flakes crushed dried chillies.
red thai small, medium hot and bright red in colour.

CHINESE COOKING WINE also known as hao hsing or chinese rice wine; made from fermented rice, wheat, sugar and salt with a 13.5 per cent alcohol content. Inexpensive and found in Asian food shops; if you can't find it, replace with mirin or sherry.

CHORIZO a sausage of Spanish origin, made from coarsely ground pork and highly seasoned with garlic and chilli.

COCONUT CREAM the first pressing from grated mature coconut flesh; available in cans and cartons.

CORIANDER also known as cilantro or chinese parsley; bright-green leafy herb with a pungent flavour; the whole plant (roots, stems and leaves) is used in Asian cooking. Also sold as seeds, whole or ground, however, these cannot be used in place of the fresh herb as the tastes are completely different.

CRÈME FRAÎCHE (minimum fat content 35%) a mature fermented cream having a slightly tangy, nutty flavour and velvety texture. Available from supermarkets.

CURRY POWDER a blend of ground spices used for convenience when making Indian food. Choose mild or hot to suit your taste.

ENDIVE, CURLY also known as frisée, a curly-leafed green vegetable, mainly used in salads.

FENNEL a white to very pale green-white, firm, crisp, roundish vegetable about 8-12cm in diameter. The bulb has a slightly sweet, anise flavour but the leaves have a much stronger taste. Also the name given to dried seeds having a licorice flavour.

FISH SAUCE also called nam pla or nuoc nam; made from pulverised salted fermented fish, usually anchovies. Has a pungent smell and strong taste, so use according to your taste .

FIVE-SPICE POWDER a fragrant mix of ground cinnamon, cloves, star anise, sichuan pepper and fennel seeds. Also known as chinese five-spice.

FLAT-LEAF PARSLEY also known as continental parsley or italian parsley.

GALANGAL also known as laos. It looks like ginger but is dense and fibrous and much harder to cut. Galangal adds a distinctive peppery flavour to food. If using in pieces, remove from the dish before serving. Fresh ginger can be substituted for fresh galangal, but the flavour of the dish will not be the same.

GINGER also known as green or root ginger; the thick gnarled root of a tropical plant.
pickled can be either pink or red coloured and is available from Asian food shops. The paper-thin shavings of ginger are pickled in a mixture of vinegar, sugar and natural colouring.

GNOCCHI Italian 'dumplings' made of potatoes, semolina or flour.

GOW GEE WRAPPERS pastry sheets, made of flour, egg and water; found in the refrigerated or freezer section of Asian food shops and many supermarkets. Wonton wrappers, spring roll or egg pastry sheets can be substituted.

HAZELNUTS also known as filberts; plump, grape-sized nuts having a brown inedible skin removed by rubbing heated nuts together vigorously in a tea-towel.

HERBS we have specified when to use fresh or dried herbs. We used dried (not ground) herbs in the proportion of 1:4 for fresh herbs; use 1 teaspoon dried herbs instead of 4 teaspoons (1 tablespoon) chopped fresh herbs.

KAFFIR LIME LEAVES also known as bai magrood, look like they are two glossy dark green leaves joined end to end, forming a rounded hourglass shape; used fresh or dried. A strip of fresh lime peel may be substituted for each kaffir lime leaf.

KALAMATA OLIVES small, sharp-tasting, brine-cured black olives.

LAKSA PASTE a bottled paste of lemon grass, chillies, galangal, shrimp paste, onions and turmeric. Commercial laksa pastes vary dramatically in their heat intensity so adjust the amount to suit your heat tolerance.

LEMON GRASS a tall, clumping, lemon-smelling and tasting, sharp-edged grass; use the white lower part of each stem.

MUSHROOMS
button small, cultivated white mushrooms with a mild flavour.
flat large, flat mushrooms with a rich earthy flavour. They are sometimes misnamed field mushrooms, which are wild mushrooms.
swiss brown also known as cremini or roman mushrooms, are light brown mushrooms having a full-bodied flavour. Button mushrooms can be substituted.

MUSTARD
dijon a pale brown, distinctively flavoured, fairly mild french mustard.
wholegrain also known as seeded. A french-style coarse-grain mustard made from crushed mustard seeds and dijon-style french mustard.

OIL
olive made from ripened olives. Extra virgin and virgin are the best, while extra light or light refers to taste rather than fat levels.
peanut pressed from ground peanuts; most commonly used oil in Asian cooking because of its high smoke point.
sesame made from roasted, crushed sesame seeds. Do not use for frying.

PALM SUGAR also known as nam tan pip, jaggery, jawa or gula melaka; made from the sap of the sugar palm tree. Usually sold in rock-hard cakes; substitute it with brown sugar, if unavailable.

PAPRIKA ground dried red capsicum (pepper), available sweet or hot.

PESTO a paste originally made from basil, oil, garlic, pine nuts and parmesan. These days, bottled versions, made from such ingredients as sun-dried tomatoes and capsicums, roasted vegetables and coriander are available from major supermarkets and deilcatessens.

PINE NUTS also known as pignoli; small, cream-coloured kernels from the cones of different varieties of pine trees.

PINK PEPPERCORNS not true peppercorns but actually the dried berry from a type of rose plant grown in Madagascar; usually sold packed in brine (occasionally found freeze-dried). They possess a distinctive pungently sweet taste that goes well with cream sauces.

PISTACHIO pale green, delicately flavoured nut inside a hard off-white shell. To peel, soak shelled nuts in boiling water for 5 minutes; drain, then pat dry with absorbent paper. Rub skins with cloth to peel.

PRESERVED LEMONS a North African specialty; lemons are quartered and preserved in salt and lemon juice. To use, remove and discard pulp, squeeze juice from rind, rinse rind well; slice thinly. Sold in Middle-Eastern food shops, major supermarkets and delicatessens.

PROSCIUTTO salt-cured, air-dried (unsmoked) pressed ham.

ROCKET also known as arugula, rugula and rucola; a peppery-tasting green leaf. Baby rocket, also known as wild rocket, is both smaller and less peppery.

SAFFRON stigma of a member of the crocus family, available in strands or ground form; imparts a yellow-orange colour to food once infused in hot water. Very expensive, it should be stored in the freezer.

SAMBAL OELEK (also ulek or olek) Indonesian in origin; a salty paste made from ground chillies.

SEAFOOD MARINARA MIX a mixture of uncooked chopped seafood available from fishmarkets and fishmongers.

SNOW PEAS also called mange tout ('eat all'). A small fresh pea that can be eaten whole, pod and all.

SOY SAUCE made from fermented soya beans. Several variations are available in most supermarkets.

STAR ANISE a dried star-shaped fruit of a tree native to China. The pods, which have an astringent aniseed or licorice flavour, are widely used in the Asian kitchen. Available whole or ground.

SWEET CHILLI SAUCE a comparatively mild, thai-style sauce made from red chillies, sugar, garlic and vinegar.

TOMATOES
cherry also known as tiny tim or tom thumb; small, round tomatoes.
paste triple-concentrated tomato puree used to add flavour to soups, casseroles and sauces.
plum also called egg or roma, smallish, oval-shaped tomatoes much used in Italian cooking and salads.
puree canned pureed tomatoes (not tomato paste). Substitute with fresh peeled and pureed tomatoes.
semi-dried partially dried tomato pieces in olive oil. Softer and juicier than sun-dried, these are not preserves so do not keep as long as sun-dried. Usually sold marinated in herbed olive oil; they are soft enough to be consumed without needing to be reconstituted.
sun-dried totally dehydrated tomatoes sold bottled in oil or packaged in plastic; they need to be reconstituted before being eaten. We used sun-dried tomatoes in oil, unless otherwise specified.

VINEGAR
balsamic authentic only from the province of Modena, Italy; aged in antique wooden casks to give the exquisite pungent flavour. It is a deep rich brown colour with a sweet and sour flavour.
rice a colourless vinegar made from fermented rice and flavoured with sugar and salt. Also known as seasoned rice vinegar.
sherry made from a blend of wines and left in wood vats to mature where they develop a rich mellow flavour.

WOMBOK also known as peking cabbage, chinese cabbage or petsai. Elongated in shape with pale green, crinkly leaves, this is the most common cabbage in South-East Asian cooking.

WONTON WRAPPERS see gow gee wrappers.

WORCESTERSHIRE SAUCE a thin, dark-brown spicy sauce that is used both as a seasoning and condiment.

ZUCCHINI also known as courgette.

conversion chart

MEASURES

One Australian metric measuring cup holds approximately 250ml; one Australian metric tablespoon holds 20ml; one Australian metric teaspoon holds 5ml.

The difference between one country's measuring cups and another's is within a two- or three-teaspoon variance, and will not affect your cooking results. North America, New Zealand and the United Kingdom use a 15ml tablespoon.

All cup and spoon measurements are level. The most accurate way of measuring dry ingredients is to weigh them. When measuring liquids, use a clear glass or plastic jug with the metric markings.

We use large eggs with an average weight of 60g.

DRY MEASURES

METRIC	IMPERIAL
15g	½oz
30g	1oz
60g	2oz
90g	3oz
125g	4oz (¼lb)
155g	5oz
185g	6oz
220g	7oz
250g	8oz (½lb)
280g	9oz
315g	10oz
345g	11oz
375g	12oz (¾lb)
410g	13oz
440g	14oz
470g	15oz
500g	16oz (1lb)
750g	24oz (1½lb)
1kg	32oz (2lb)

LIQUID MEASURES

METRIC	IMPERIAL
30ml	1 fluid oz
60ml	2 fluid oz
100ml	3 fluid oz
125ml	4 fluid oz
150ml	5 fluid oz (¼ pint/1 gill)
190ml	6 fluid oz
250ml	8 fluid oz
300ml	10 fluid oz (½ pint)
500ml	16 fluid oz
600ml	20 fluid oz (1 pint)
1000ml (1 litre)	1¾ pints

LENGTH MEASURES

METRIC	IMPERIAL
3mm	⅛in
6mm	¼in
1cm	½in
2cm	¾in
2.5cm	1in
5cm	2in
6cm	2½in
8cm	3in
10cm	4in
13cm	5in
15cm	6in
18cm	7in
20cm	8in
23cm	9in
25cm	10in
28cm	11in
30cm	12in (1ft)

OVEN TEMPERATURES

These oven temperatures are only a guide for conventional ovens. For fan-forced ovens, check the manufacturer's manual.

	°C (CELSIUS)	°F (FAHRENHEIT)	GAS MARK
Very slow	120	250	½
Slow	150	275-300	1-2
Moderately slow	160	325	3
Moderate	180	350-375	4-5
Moderately hot	200	400	6
Hot	220	425-450	7-8
Very hot	240	475	9

index

If you like this cookbook, you'll love these...

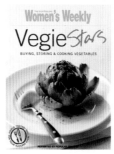

These are just a small selection of titles available in
The Australian Women's Weekly range on sale at selected
newsagents, supermarkets or online at www.acpbooks.com.au

also available in bookstores...

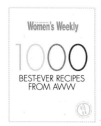

ACP BOOKS

General manager Christine Whiston

Editor-in-chief Susan Tomnay

Creative director & designer Hieu Chi Nguyen

Art director Hannah Blackmore

Senior editor Wendy Bryant

Food director Pamela Clark

Test Kitchen manager + nutritional information Belinda Farlow

Director of sales Brian Cearnes

Marketing manager Bridget Cody

Communications & brand manager Xanthe Roberts

Senior business analyst Rebecca Varela

Circulation manager Jama Mclean

Operations manager David Scotto

Production manager Victoria Jefferys

European rights enquiries Laura Bamford lbamford@acpuk.com

ACP Books are published by ACP Magazines a division of
PBL Media Pty Limited

PBL Media, Chief Executive Officer Ian Law

Publishing & sales director, Women's lifestyle Lynette Phillips

Group editorial director, Women's lifestyle Pat Ingram

Marketing director, Women's lifestyle Matthew Dominello

Commercial manager, Women's lifestyle Seymour Cohen

Research director, Women's lifestyle Justin Stone

Produced by ACP Books, Sydney.

Published by ACP Books, a division of ACP Magazines Ltd,
54 Park St, Sydney; GPO Box 4088, Sydney, NSW 2001.
phone (02) 9282 8618; fax (02) 9267 9438;
acpbooks@acpmagazines.com.au; www.acpbooks.com.au

Printed by Dai Nippon in Korea.

Australia Distributed by Network Services,
phone +61 2 9282 8777; fax +61 2 9264 3278;
networkweb@networkservicescompany.com.au

United Kingdom Distributed by Australian Consolidated Press (UK),
phone (01604) 642 200; fax (01604) 642 300; books@acpuk.com

New Zealand Distributed by Netlink Distribution Company,
phone (9) 366 9966; ask@ndc.co.nz

South Africa Distributed by PSD Promotions,
phone (27 11) 392 6065/6/7; fax (27 11) 392 6079/80;
orders@psdprom.co.za

Canada Distributed by Publishers Group Canada
phone (800) 663 5714; fax (800) 565 3770; service@raincoast.com

Title: 100 pasta favourites / food director Pamela Clark.

ISBN: 978 1 86396 947 5 (pbk.)

Notes: Includes index.

Subjects: Cookery (Pasta)

Other Authors/Contributors: Clark, Pamela.

Dewey Number: 641.822

© ACP Magazines Ltd 2009

ABN 18 053 273 546

To order books, phone 136 116 (within Australia)
or order online at www.acpbooks.com.au

Send recipe enquiries to:
recipeenquiries@acpmagazines.com.au